W9-CYG-975

WORDS
OF
WISDOM

BEGINNING BUDDHISM

By
Venerable Master Hsuan Hua

Volume One

WORDS OF WISDOM

BEGINNING BUDDHISM

Buddhist Text Translation Society
Dharma Realm Buddhist University
Dharma Realm Buddhist Association

Buddhist Text Translation Society
1777 Murchison Drive,
Burlingame, CA 94010-4504

WORDS OF WISDOM

A series by Venerable Master Hsuan Hua

V. 1 Beginning Buddhism
V. 2 Chan Meditation
V. 3 The Way
V. 4 Developing Virtue
V. 5 Daily Practice
V. 6 Roots of Goodness

Series ISBN 0-88139-311-8

Cover design: Vicki Chien

Published by: Buddhist Text Translation Society
Dharma Realm Buddhist University
Dharma Realm Buddhist Association

WORDS OF WISDOM
BEGINNING BUDDHISM - Vol. 1

Published and translated by:
Buddhist Text Translation Society
1777 Murchison Drive,
Burlingame, CA 94010-4504

Printed in Taiwan
First Edition - 2003

10 09 08 07 06 05 04 03 1 2 3 4 5 6 7 8

Library of Congress Cataloging-in-Publication Data

Hsuan Hua, 1908-
Beginning Buddhism / by Venerable Master Hsuan Hua; translated by Buddhist Text Translation Society.— 1st ed.
p. cm. — (Words of wisdom)

ISBN 0-88139-302-9
1. Buddhism. 2. Conduct of life. I. Buddhist Text Translation Society. II. Title. III. Series.

BQ4012.H76 2003
294.3—dc21

2003005908

BEGINNING BUDDHISM - Vol. 1

WHAT IS BUDDHISM?

Cultivating the Way simply means to "turn ourselves around."

WHAT is Buddhadharma? Buddhadharma is simply worldly dharma, but it's a variety of worldly dharma that many people are unwilling to use. Most people keep themselves busy running around and are constantly hurried and agitated. The primal source of all this activity is selfishness, motivated by a concern to protect one's life and possessions. Buddhadharma, on the other hand, is unselfish and public-spirited, and springs from a wish to benefit others. As we learn the Buddhadharma, our every action gradually comes to include in its scope a concern for others. The ego gradually loses its importance. We should give up our own interests in service to others, and avoid bringing affliction to others. These are the hallmarks of the Buddhadharma. But most people fail to clearly understand these basic ideas. When that lack of understanding reaches even Buddhist circles, then struggle and contention, troubles and hassles, quarrels and strife may result.

If that happens, then how Buddhists behave will not be all that different from the way most anyone behaves. Sometimes the relationships within Buddhist groups don't even measure up to the standards of ordinary social conduct. That occurs when people study Buddhism on the one hand and create offenses on the other. They do good deeds, and in the next breath destroy the merit and virtue they've earned. Instead of advancing the cause of Buddhism, such behavior actually harms it. The Buddha referred to such people as "parasites on the lion, feeding off the lion's flesh."

We Buddhist disciples cannot expect any results from our cultivation if we're selfish and profiteering, unable to put things down and see through our attachments. The motto of Buddhists must be:

Let me truly recognize my own faults,
And not discuss others' shortcomings.
Others' faults are just my own:
Being one with all things is Great Compassion.

If we want to thoroughly understand the truths of Buddhism, then we must first cultivate patience and giving. Then we can come to accomplishment. We must turn ourselves around and be different from ordinary people. We can no longer flow along with the turbid currents of life. Cultivating the Way simply means "turning ourselves around." This means simply "giving desirable situations and benefits to other people, and keeping the unfavorable situations for ourselves." We renounce the petty self in order to bring to perfection the greater self.

All disciples who have taken refuge with me are like the flesh and blood of my own body. No matter which piece of flesh is severed from my body, it hurts me just the same. No matter where I bleed, the wound injures my constitution. Because of this, all of you must be united. To make Buddhism expand and flourish, you must take a loss in situations where most people are unable to. You must endure the insults that ordinary people find unendurable. Expand the measure of your minds, and be true in your actions. When you're not trying to be true, the Buddhas and Bodhisattvas are aware of it. No one can cheat them. Each of you should examine your own faults and earnestly correct the flaws in your character. Truly recognize where in the past you've been upside-down and where your behavior has departed from principle. Be honest, forget about yourself, and work for the sake of all of Buddhism and all of society.

No matter where you look in the world, every organization and every society has its own complications and power struggles. At the Way-places, schools, and institutes that belong to the Dharma Realm Buddhist Association, we must correct these faults. Naturally, we can't expect perfection immediately, but we can hope to improve step by step. We can change things until we reach the ultimate point of perfection. Then in thought after thought, we must preserve this wholesome behavior and maintain our resolve and purpose as we go about disseminating Buddhism, so that its light spreads far and wide. All disciples of the Buddha share this responsibility equally. We must think, "If Buddhism fails to flourish, I haven't fulfilled my responsibility." Don't pass your duty to others. If we can shoulder our responsibility in this way, then in the near future, Buddhism will certainly expand and spread to every corner of the world!

As Buddhist disciples, do we seek the Buddhas' aid every day? Do we pray that the Buddha will help us get rich, help us rise to power, or help us develop wisdom? Are we concerned only with personal advantages? Do we forget all about making a contribution to Buddhism? Have we brought forth a genuine resolve or not? It is right at this point that we must reflect inwardly. When we took refuge with the Triple Jewel, we made the four vast vows of Bodhisattvas:

1. Living beings are numberless, I vow to save them all. Ask yourself, "Have I saved any living beings?" If so, then why not save a few more? And if not, then all the more reason to quickly resolve to rescue living beings.

2. Afflictions are infinite, I vow to cut them off. There is a limitless quantity of afflictions, but we must reverse them, transform them into Bodhi. "Have I reversed them?" If not, then quickly turn them over right away!

3. Dharma-doors are measureless, I vow to learn them all. Ask yourself, "Have I learned any of the Buddhadharma? Have I brought forth the slightest bit of strength for Buddhism? Have I been too rigid and inflexible in my study of the teachings? Is my study of the various Dharma-doors off and on?"

4. The Buddha's Way is supreme, I vow to realize it. There is no dharma on earth that surpasses the Buddha's Way, nor one that is more ultimate. Have I really made a resolve to accomplish Buddhahood? What's more, we shouldn't resolve to accomplish Buddhahood for ourselves alone, but to take all living beings across to Buddhahood.

In the past, Shakyamuni Buddha "cultivated blessings and wisdom for three great innumerable eons, and developed the fine features and hallmarks for one hundred eons." He gave up his life for half a verse of Dharma. How great his spirit was! His sincerity in seeking the Dharma was truly noble.

We should all imitate his model of vigor. Don't fail to gain any genuine benefit from the Dharma. Don't fail to experience the greatness of the spirit of the Buddhadharma. Be sure not to place yourselves outside the Buddhadharma, without being able to deeply enter it.

Our attitude should be, "If Buddhism is going to flourish, then it must begin with me." What we need are true hearts, endowed with a genuine spirit of devotion to the Buddhadharma. Work hard and break free of the small circles that you've drawn around yourselves. Take the entire Dharma Realm as your own body! Let all of empty space be your field of action! This means, "bringing forth thoughts that linger nowhere." If every person would really do this, then Buddhism could truly flourish in this country.

THE BUDDHA-NATURE INHERENT IN US ALL

There can be endless births and infinite transformations in the world, all because of the Buddha-Nature

IN THE VERY beginning, the universe was nebulous and indistinguishable. As Heaven and Earth evolved, there were no living creatures. The world as we know it now wasn't identifiable then. There was basically nothing at all. Later, during the phase of becoming, living beings came into being bit by bit. Ultimately, where did human beings come from? Some people say they evolved from apes. But what did the apes evolve from? If it was possible for apes to turn into people in the past, why can't they change into people now? Couldn't we just as well suppose that people evolved from mice or from caterpillars? How do we know that mice didn't evolve from people?

Who is the first ancestor of all the flying, swimming, and roaming creatures, as well as all plants? What is the origin of birds in the sky; fish, turtles, shrimp, crabs, and other creatures in the water; people and other creatures endowed with blood and breath; and flowers, grasses, trees, and all other plants? The Buddha-nature is.

Endless births and infinite transformations that occur all come about because of the Buddha-nature. If the Buddha-nature did not exist, everything would cease to be. The Buddha-nature alone endures without perishing throughout ages and exists eternally in every ancestral line.

The Ten Dharma Realms transform and come into being because of the Buddha-nature. The Ten Dharma Realms are not apart from a single thought. That single thought is the Buddha-nature. People are endowed with the Buddha-nature and when people fall lower in the cycle of rebirth, they can become animals. The theory of the Ten Dharma Realms is a very clear explanation of how things are.

Ultimately, how did people come into being? Let's look at how chickens came into being. Which came first, the chicken or the egg? Without a chicken, there's no egg. Without an egg, there's no chicken. That "chicken-egg theory" has no final answer.

A similar theory can apply to people. Let's consider male and female. Which came first, man or woman? To say the man was first won't work because a man is born from a woman's womb. To say that the woman was first won't work because the male element is needed for conception to occur. Because it was so long ago, people have forgotten just how humans came into being.

All phenomena come from the Buddha-nature. They keep coming into being and ceasing to be, in an endless series of births and transformations that are ever-increasing like bugs born in rice. By the way, that's case of something insentient producing something sentient. By the same principle, the Buddha-nature can transform nothing into something, producing all living beings and humankind. The theory that humans evolved from apes is not substantial. You can see that the people of different countries have different appearances—there are black, yellow, white, and red-skinned people. What did they evolve from? You can talk about it this way and that, but you'll never find an answer. Understanding the Buddha-nature is a reliable way of explaining how humans evolved, but few people have the wisdom to reach that level of understanding.

People came into being from nothingness, and all other living beings are that way, too. Cultivation involves turning existence into nothingness, returning to the origin, and going back to the inherent Buddha-nature. "What use is that?" you ask. Well, what use is your being a person? If you can return to your inherent Buddha-nature, you will quickly be able to accomplish the Buddha Way. The Buddha-nature exists eternally. Even if all living beings die, the Buddha-nature will never perish.

Earth Store Bodhisattva's vows inspire me to try to explain the principles involved in becoming a person and behaving like a human being—how "nothing turns into something, and something turns into nothing." If you don't believe that principle, then how do you explain bugs getting born in rice? People in the world are also like bugs, except that they have a higher level of perceptive ability and a soul. But they are still a long way from the Buddha. Comparing people to the Buddha is just like comparing bugs to people.

If you understand that, then you will be able to cultivate. In cultivation, we must be as steady as a balanced scale, calm and peaceful, with no waves in our nature. If we are really ready to accept Buddhism, then we can discuss Buddhism with each other, and together we can investigate how to cultivate. If anyone is not ready to accept Buddhism, but is still involved in seeking name and gain, and cannot put down wealth, sex, fame, food, and sleep or anything else for that matter, then how can such a person learn the truths of Buddhism and cultivation of the Way? Let's all wake up!

A talk given on September 13, 1982

BUDDHISM REVEALS HOW FAIR THINGS ARE

The retributions we receive for every good thing we do and every crime we commit will be absolutely fair.

THE TEACHINGS of Buddhism are subtle and wonderful. Those who are Buddhist may not detect any advantage in that, and those who are not Buddhist may not feel any disadvantage in that. However, Buddhism clarifies that the retributions we receive for every good thing we do and every crime we commit will not be off by a hairsbreadth. The greatest freedom and equality can also be found within Buddhism. Buddhism is not biased in the least.

What attests to Buddhism's equality? Anyone who truly resolves to cultivate, be they a hungry ghost, hell-being, evil spirit, ferocious beast, wicked person, or bad person, has the same potential. It is said that "a turn of the head is the other shore," meaning that anyone who decides to, can become a Buddha. Buddhism differs from other beliefs in that it does not consider anyone to be eternally bad and beyond redemption. The teachings of Buddhism stress that even ferocious and wild beasts can be saved.

During the Ming dynasty, Great Master Lianchi accepted a tiger as his disciple. This tiger disciple accompanied the Master everywhere, protecting him. Since tigers are known to be vicious beasts, everyone who saw this tiger was terrified. Thereupon Great Master Lianchi told the tiger to walk backwards instead of forward. When the tiger did that, people who saw it coming felt reassured that the beast was tame and no longer were afraid of it. The tiger went everywhere to raise funds for the Great Master. People all crowded in to make offerings when they saw this good tiger coming. Buddhism makes it clear that tigers and such can also take refuge with the Triple Jewel, protect the Buddhadharma and become Buddhas.

Buddhism gives people the greatest freedom, because in Buddhism, people are exhorted to practice good deeds and abstain from evil deeds. If we do evil, we ourselves must suffer the retribution. The teachings of Buddhism do not force people to do good. That's because everything is made from the mind alone. The heavens and the hells are created based on people's thoughts and the force of their karma. Buddhism teaches people to "Abstain from all evil and offer up all good conduct," and explains how accurate the law of cause and effect is. Buddhism teaches people to recognize the truth and transcend the cycle of birth and death.

OUR GOAL IN CULTIVATING THE WAY IS BUDDHAHOOD

We must not fail to recognize right from wrong. We should clearly distinguish black from white.

WHY CULTIVATE the Way? We cultivate in order to become Buddhas. How do we become Buddhas? The first step is to not do any evil deeds and to do many good deeds. The second step is to diligently cultivate precepts, concentration, and wisdom and to put an end to greed, hatred, and delusion. The third step is to make the great commitment to realize Bodhi and to cultivate the Bodhisattva Path. Before we realized Buddhahood, we choose a broad, level, great bright road to travel on. We should not risk taking short cuts through treacherous, narrow bypaths. We could easily lose our direction. Pay heed to this! Take care!

Real cultivators rely on the Dharma in their cultivation. They fear no pain, and they fear no difficulty, but advance courageously all the way to Buddhahood. A saying goes:

> *Grind the iron pillar down to sewing-needle size.*
> *Your efforts will bear fruit when the work matures.*

Applying maximum effort will naturally bring us to Buddhahood. We shouldn't show off, trying to make people think we are special. We shouldn't brag about our virtue. People who have those problems will take forever to attain Buddhahood.

If we perfect the ability to use the Five Spiritual Eyes, then we'll be able to see how all Buddhas throughout the ten directions cultivate to attain Buddhahood. We'll see how all Bodhisattvas of the ten directions cultivate to attain Bodhisattvahood. And we'll see how all Arhats in the ten directions cultivate to attain Arhatship. We will be able to perceive such states in a single glance.

People who perceive with the Five Spiritual Eyes can instantly understand the ultimate reality of all dharmas and comprehend the entire Twelve Divisions and Three Treasuries of the Canon the Buddha spoke.

The verse for taking refuge with the Triple Jewel says:

To the Buddha I return and rely,
Vowing that all living beings
Understand the Great Way profoundly,
And bring forth the Bodhi-mind.

To the Dharma I return and rely,
Vowing that all living beings
Deeply enter the Sutra-treasury,
And have wisdom like the sea.

To the Sangha I return and rely,
Vowing that all living beings
Form together a great assembly,
One and all in harmony.

If we can "deeply enter the Sutra-treasury and have wisdom like the sea," there will be nothing we do not fathom, nothing we do not understand, nothing we do not know, and nothing we do not see. That describes great and penetrating enlightenment. We should not miss out on the great because we cling to the small. We should not allow our greed for petty states of mind to obscure the Great, All-encompassing, Mirror-like Wisdom that is inherently ours. If we do, we won't be able to deeply enter the Sutra-treasury and have wisdom like the sea.

People who realize great wisdom definitely do not crave petty states of mind. Someone who is greedy for petty states of mind is someone who does not clearly distinguish truth from falsehood. Such a person mistakes brass for gold and assumes that gold is brass. Such a person would rather have a piece of crystal than a diamond. Why? Because he can't distinguish between true and false.

Cultivation of the Way requires proper knowledge and proper views. You must not confuse right and wrong. You have to distinguish black from white clearly. Avoid mistaking fish-eyes for pearls. Don't march in place just to kill time. Otherwise, you will acquire wrong knowledge and views and will never succeed in cultivation of Buddhahood.

What are proper knowledge and views? Simply put, if we can get rid of the three poisons in our thoughts, then our body and mind will be pure. Our wisdom will reveal itself, and we'll be able to light up the darkness of ignorance and cure the feverish illness of afflictions. It is then that we attain the positions of sagehood. I hope that all of you will advance towards that goal!

EVERYTHING IS AN EXPRESSION OF DHARMA

If we understand, we can let things go. If we don't understand, we will remain attached.

THE AVATAMSAKA SUTRA says, "The Buddhas use billions of different sounds to proclaim the wonderful Dharma for living beings." We realize that in fact all sounds in the world are expressions of Dharma. Another saying goes:

> *The sounds of the brooks come from*
> *the vast, long tongue.*
> *The hues of the mountains are none other*
> *than the pure body.*

The sounds of the streams and creeks come from the vast, long tongue of the Buddha and are proclamations of the wonderful Dharma. The hues of the green mountains are all the pure Dharma-body, delighting those who see them. If we understand this principle, then absolutely everything in the world is an expression of Dharma.

Good people express good Dharma for us, and bad people express bad Dharma for us. Horses express the Dharma of being a horse, and cows express the Dharma of being a cow, enabling us to understand how they got to be horses and cows. As a matter of fact, in their previous lives, horses and cows were probably people who were unfilial to their parents and disrespectful to their teachers. Perhaps they refused to listen to the admonishments of their parents and teachers, and even turned their backs to them. Even as animals in this life their behavior hasn't changed much.

In general, if we observe the five precepts and practice the ten good deeds, then we can be born in the human realm or the heavens. If we harbor greed, anger and delusion in our minds, then we will fall into the three evil paths.

Cats catch mice, tigers prey on rabbits. The weak are eaten by the strong. All those things express the Dharma. Each event has its own cause and effect, its own standing, and its own wonderful Dharma. Professors express the Dharma of professors, and students express the Dharma of students. Bhikshus express the Dharma of Bhikshus, and Bhikshunis express the Dharma of Bhikshunis. Sentient beings are expressing the Dharma, and insentient things are also expressing the Dharma. If we can recognize that, then the green mountains, the white clouds, the yellow flowers, and the green bamboo are all expressions of Dharma. All the myriad things and creatures are expressions of Dharma.

Robbers loot the wealth and property of other people because those people robbed them in previous lives, and they are now collecting the debt. If they weren't robbed in the past, and they rob the wealth and property of others now, they will be robbed in the future in order to pay their debt. Such is the principle of retribution within the cycle of cause and effect.

Therefore, people should act in an upright way, be altruistic and unselfish. Don't try to take advantage of situations. If you gain advantages by forcing it, you are actually taking a loss. It is said, "taking a loss is actually gaining an advantage." Keep that in mind, and don't forget it! If you're not supposed to gain an advantage, but you insist on getting it, you will just lose capital. If you're supposed to gain an advantage, and you don't try to get it, then you are putting a deposit in the bank. Thus, each person should stand in his proper place and do his best to fulfill his obligations. This is also expressing the Dharma.

The emerald-green bamboo is just the Dharma-body.
The thriving yellow flowers are nothing but Prajna.

That's how we should contemplate all things. If we understand, we can let them go. If we don't understand, we will remain attached.

THE NATURE, CONSCIOUSNESS, INTENT, AND MIND

If you can remain unperturbed by external states, then you are cultivating. If you are turned by external states, then you will fall.

Q: WHAT ARE the differences between the nature, the consciousness, the intent, and the mind?

A: Newborn babies are innocent and true. They have no concept of self, others, living beings, or lifespans. That quality is their nature. As soon as they start to nurse, their consciousness becomes active. Eventually, they become aware that without clothes they will feel cold and embarrassed. When they become aware of hunger, thirst, cold, and heat, their intent is forming. Then when they mature and start wanting to acquire material things, they are using their mind.

Those are the four basic aspects of our minds, but they could also be described as one, because they are interrelated and cannot be separated. They are of the same family. Although there are four names, their fundamental nature is the same. The reason for that basic defilement is karma.

To expand upon this topic we can ask what a Buddha is? Our nature is the Buddha. What is our spirit? Our consciousness is our spirit. Our intent is the distinction-making mind, and the mind itself is what constantly engages in idle thinking.

Further, the nature is originally perfect and bright, with no concept of self or others, and no falling into a second or third level of truth. But as soon as consciousness emerges, one falls into a second or third level of truth and begins making discriminations. The intent, also called the sixth consciousness, increases the distinction-making. It is relatively turbid, while the seventh and eighth consciousnesses are more pure.

There are eight kinds of consciousness: the six consciousnesses of the eye, ear, nose, tongue, body, and intent, and the seventh and eighth consciousnesses. Fundamentally, consciousness is not of eight kinds, although there are eight kinds in name. We could say that there is a single headquarters with eight departments under it. Although there are eight departments, they are controlled by the headquarters. The eight are one, and the one is eight. The eight don't contradict the one, and the one doesn't contradict the eight. From the one, the eight come forth. From eight, they can also return to one. That's the consciousness.

The intent is the discriminating mind, the sixth consciousness. Not only does the mind make discriminations, it is filled with idle thoughts. The six consciousnesses can also be said to be a perceptive nature. That is, from the six sense organs—eyes, ears, nose, tongue, body, and intent—the functions of seeing, hearing, smelling, tasting, feeling, and knowing arise. When people commit offenses, they do it with the six sense organs. When they cultivate, they also do it with the six sense organs. Anyone who remains unperturbed by external states is cultivating. Being turned by them will cause a fall.

WHEN WE ATTAIN THE ONE, ALL THINGS WILL BE DONE

Any person who understands the Zero can cultivate and realize the fruition

All dharmas arise from conditions;
All dharmas cease with conditions.
Our Buddha, the great Shramana,
Always speaks in this way.

ALL DHARMAS arise from causes and conditions and cease because of causes and conditions. This principle, which governs rebirth, is also the principle that when something reaches its extreme, it will reverse itself. Extreme misfortune will bring prosperity. The same principle applies to all the dualities in this world.

With dualities, when good reaches an extreme, it becomes bad. When something bad goes to its extreme, something good will come of it. At birth we are good, but by the time we die, we may have become bad. The same principle applies to coming into being, dwelling, change, and extinction. After something comes into being, it dwells, then undergoes change, and finally ceases to be.

Birth, aging, sickness, and death also follow this principle. After we are born, we gradually grow old, and in old age we contract sicknesses. Sickness then brings about death. These are all conditions.

Everyone undergoes birth and is glad to be born; everyone must die, but everyone fears death. If you are neither glad to be born nor afraid to die, you have samadhi power. Why do people fear ghosts? Because ghosts are grotesque and frightening, menacing and capable of killing people. Fear of ghosts is a form of the fear of death. If you didn't fear death, you wouldn't fear anything. You wouldn't be afraid of ghosts, spirits, goblins, demons, monsters, or anything at all. If you are afraid of something, you cannot be proper. You can attain proper samadhi and reception only if you have no fear. A person who possesses samadhi power has the attitude:

Even if I meet with a knife's point,
I am always completely tranquil.
If I am given a poisonous drug,
I am still totally at ease.

The meaning is, if someone were to slice this person's head off with a knife, he wouldn't mind too much. He wouldn't be moved. Why not? Because he's already put an end to birth and death. He has done what had to be done and will not undergo rebirth. When we attain the One, all things are done.

However, attaining the One is not enough. We must find a way to get back to the origin and turn it into a Zero. The Zero is an ineffably wonderful principle. Any person who understands the Zero can cultivate and realize the fruition. How can you understand the Zero? You must first understand the One. When we attain the One, all things are done. That is beyond the marks of speech, words, and conditions of the mind. Sweep away all dharmas, and separate from all marks. Not a single dharma exists; all dharmas are empty. If you want to attain this kind of state and realize this principle, you must first attain the One. You shouldn't think the One is so simple.

> *When heaven attains the One, it becomes clear;*
> *When earth attains the One, it becomes peaceful;*
> *When a person attains the One, he becomes a sage.*

Why is heaven able to shelter the myriad creatures and things? Because it has attained the One. Why is earth able to nurture the myriad things? Because it has attained the One. If the earth lost the One, there would be landslides, earthquakes, tidal waves, and all kinds of disasters. Wherever the One is lost, there will be incessant calamities. If the One is not lost, the earth will be peaceful and secure.

When a person attains the One, he becomes a sage. If a person really attains the One, he will escape rebirth, realize sagehood, and open up his wisdom. When people have lost the One, they undergo rebirth in the six paths and suffer all kinds of afflictions and ignorance. The eighty-four thousand afflictions all come about because we have lost the One. If we attain the One, then afflictions will turn into Bodhi and birth and death will become Nirvana; it's as easy as turning over our hand, not difficult at all. So why haven't people been able turn afflictions into Bodhi, and birth and death into Nirvana? It's because they've lost the One, and on gone to two, three,..., ten. From ten they go to limitless powers of ten, and hundreds of thousands of afflictions come up. Thus the One is very important. But once someone loses the One, it's not easy to regain it. And going from the One back to the origin, to Zero, is even more difficult.

Here's another simple analogy. When is it called the One? When is it called the Zero? During the period from ages one to fourteen for girls and ages one to sixteen for boys, the One is not yet lost. When is it the Zero? From the time of conception until birth is the stage of the Zero, because there are no random thoughts, afflictions, greed, anger, or delusion. But once a child learns to eat, greed for food arises when it feels hungry; and then greed, anger, and delusion all ensue. Nonetheless, at that point a person still haven't lost the One. At the start of your life as a person, the Zero becomes the One. The One is still very complete, and it is the beginning of everything. However, as you experience the changes of people and things, more things are added on top of the One, so it becomes two; two becomes three; three becomes four,...and it keeps increasing. The more it increases, the heavier the burden gets, and the more dull-witted you become.

The nature is the Zero, and the Zero is the nature. The Zero and the nature have nothing to them at all:

> *Originally there's not a single thing;*
> *Where can the dust alight?*

We want to cultivate until we become as innocent as a newborn baby. Our mind should be empty, like a child's. We should return to youth in our old age. However, that doesn't mean we should start drinking our mother's milk again. Rather, it means we should cast out all thoughts of greed, anger, delusion, pride, and doubt. To do that is to return to our source. Our thoughts and outlook become as a child's are: innocent and pure, without the slightest bit of laziness, greed for advantages, or criticism of other's faults. At that point, we understand that originally there's not a single thing, so where can the dust alight?

If we can understand that principle and cultivate with it in mind, then we can truly become enlightened. Why do we listen to lectures on the Sutras? Because we want to return to the origin. Why do we cultivate? Because we want to get back to the source. We want to clean up all our miscellaneous garbage, so that we don't need to spend all our time on the question of self and others.

It shouldn't be that when someone talks badly about us, we get upset and cannot bear it, or that if someone were to touch even one hair on our bodies, the pain would sear our hearts, or that if we could benefit the world by pulling out even one hair, we wouldn't do it. With such selfishness, we won't be able to cultivate.

A cultivator should not have the mark of self, the mark of others, the mark of living beings, or the mark of lifespans. Not having the mark of self doesn't mean that when it's time to work, we make everyone else work. Not having the mark of others doesn't mean when it's time to eat, we say, "I have no mark of others, so it's no problem if I eat more." Or perhaps when someone is fighting, we don't help resolve it, claiming that we have no mark of living beings. Or when there's meat to eat, someone may justify eating it by saying that there's no mark of lifespans. Those are wrong views. Those are all improper ways of thinking. What's the right way?

1. Have no mark of self: We should not be arrogant, and not scheme for our own benefit.

2. Have no mark of others: We should not impede or obstruct other people. If something does not benefit others, don't do it.

3. Have no mark of living beings: We should regard all creatures as being of the same substance.

4. Have no mark of a lifespan: We should recognize that every person and every creature has the right to live. We should not take the lives of other people or other beings.

So in cultivation, we should never seek anything for ourselves or scheme for our own benefit. We should always try to think on behalf of others.

A talk given at noon on December 5, 1982

THE TAO

If we want to return to the origin, we must go from the One back to the Zero. Returning to the Zero, we find out who we are.

FISH LIVE in the water, but don't know that they are in water. People live surrounded by air, but cannot see the air. Although the air is invisible, we cannot say it doesn't exist. Fish cannot see the water, but they cannot survive outside of it.

In the human realm, there is air. In the heavens, there is a spiritual energy, a spiritual nature. And in the state of the Buddhas, there is the Buddha-nature. Although the Buddha-nature and spiritual nature cannot be seen, sages cannot be without them. Without that spiritual energy, the gods would fall into the lower realms. Without the Buddha-nature, there would be no Buddhas. These are all ineffably wonderful states. When we cultivate, we want to cultivate the great Tao which has no form or sentiment, the great Tao which is nameless. Lao Zi said in the *Classic of Purity and Stillness*,

> *The great Tao is formless; it nurtures heaven and earth.*

The great Tao is emotionless; it moves the sun and moon
in their orbits.
The great Tao is nameless; it causes the myriad things to grow.
I do not know how to describe it, so I merely call it the Tao.

At the top of the Chinese character for Tao are two short strokes, representing yin and yang. These two strokes are the inversion of the two strokes used to form the character for "person." This represents that for a person to cultivate the Tao, he must undergo an inversion. He must go against the current. Going along the current is what perpetuates birth and death; going against it brings Nirvana. The character for "going against," also has those two strokes on top that represent a "person." Each person must decide whether to go along or to oppose the current.

Beneath the two strokes top strokes in Tao is a horizontal line—the character for "one." Where do we find the Tao of being a person? We start with One, the basic substance of all numbers. Where did the One come from? Zero. Zero has no inside or outside, no beginning or end; it sweeps away all dharmas and is apart from all appearances. "Expand it, and it fills the universe; roll it up, and it hides away secretly." The Zero is the beginning of all things. To put it more plainly, the Zero is our inherent Buddha-nature. It is the great, bright, perfect treasury of light. It can be tinier than a speck of dust, or greater than the Dharma Realm. It can be limitlessly great and limitlessly small; it has no bounds.

When people do not follow the rules, the Zero breaks up and turns into One. When there is only Zero, there are no numbers. The numbers start with One. In the beginning, there is only the round, bright circle, and then it turns into the One, which is both yin and yang. "One yin and one yang make the Tao. Excessive yin or excessive yang causes sickness."

The middle part of Tao has the character for "self." Cultivation of the Tao must begin with One, and with searching for one's own self. The character for "self" has the character for "eye" in it. This tells us to look within, to turn our eyes inwards, not to look outwards.

Finally, the symbol at the left and bottom of Tao represents "walking." Putting all those elements together gives us the character Tao—"path." It becomes the Tao, or Path, only when it is walked. A path goes from one place to another. People form a path by walking it; to walk the spiritual path, we must practice with serious effort. If we want to return to the origin, we must go from One back to Zero.

When the One is attained,
All things are settled.

When we return to the Zero, we find out who we are.

A talk given on October 10, 1982

RETURN TO NOTHINGNESS

When we reach nothingness, we regain our true identity.

IN BUDDHISM we talk about returning to the origin. We want to return to the way we were originally. What were things like originally? There was nothing at all! Now we want to go back to that state of nothingness.

If we have even a particle of attachment, we have obstructions. With obstructions, we are not able to escape the Triple Realm. Therefore, it's necessary to break through all attachments. When we reach the point of having no attachments, we regain our true being.

Right now, we want there to be something, but there's nothing. When we reach the point of not wanting anything, everything will be ours. Our wisdom will appear, our spiritual powers will become evident and their wonderful function will be obvious. Why don't you have wisdom and spiritual powers right now? It is because you keep going around collecting dung. You don't want gold or diamonds; you don't want your inherent treasures either. You've thrown those away, and instead go around collecting dung, thinking you're being really clever! In fact, you're being as foolish as can be!

A talk given on March 10, 1977

ACCEPTING BUDDHISM WITHOUT FEAR, JOY, OR SORROW

Over a long journey, a horse's stamina is tested. After a long time, a person's mind can be seen.

PEOPLE who study Buddhism cannot learn all there is to know about Buddhism in just a day and night. One must gradually experience the principles of Buddhism over a long period of time. After cultivating according to the teachings for a long time, one will have some attainment.

Those who truly understand Buddhism will not be frightened by what they learn, nor be prone to laughter or tears. Buddhism is about the way things are and there is nothing to be frightened of. Nor is there anything to cry or laugh about. One should remain in a state of unmoving suchness and be clear and lucid at all times. That is how we should use our basic nature in absorbing the Dharma.

THOROUGHLY UNDERSTANDING CAUSE AND EFFECT

Sages cultivate in order to fathom the process of cause and effect. Ordinary people continue to create causes and undergo effects.

THE AVATAMSAKA *Sutra* says:

They fully realize that the various differences among beings
Arise entirely from distinctions in their thinking and activities.
Contemplating thus, they perceive with clarity
The nature of all dharmas without harming it.
The wise ones fathom the Dharma of all Buddhas.
They dedicate the merit from their practice of it,
Empathizing with all beings,
And thus enabling them to properly contemplate dharmas as they actually are.

Beings become deluded, create karma, and undergo retribution. They plant causes and then reap the corresponding results. This is a natural principle. If they plant the causes for being someone Buddhas, they reap the result of Buddhahood. If they plant the causes for being Bodhisattvas, they reap the result of

Bodhisattvahood. If they plant the causes for being someone Enlightened by Conditions, they become someone Enlightened by Conditions. If they plant the causes for being Hearers, they become Hearers. Those are the Four Sagely Realms.

The Six Common Realms are the Three Good Realms of gods, humans, and *asuras,* and the Three Evil Realms of animals, hungry ghosts, and hell-beings. In general, if one plants the causes for the Three Good Realms, one is reborn in these realms. The same applies to the Three Evil Realms. The principle of cause and effect is never off by the least bit. It is not a supersition.

Not knowing the seriousness of cause and effect, deluded people casually make mistakes in cause and effect or even deny the law of cause and effect. Wise people, knowing that the law of cause and effect relentlessly metes out the deserved retribution, dare not make mistakes in cause and effect. They always consider carefully before doing anything. Sages cultivate in order to understand the process of cause and effect. Ordinary people continue to create causes and undergo effects. Originally their offenses did not exist until they committed them. Once they have committed them, they refuse to acknowledge them as offenses, insisting they have done nothing wrong. Being devoid of shame and conscience compounds their offenses beyond the point of forgiveness.

Beings are different in various ways, including the good and bad seeds they possess. Each being creates its karma and undergoes its individual retribution. This process evolves from distinctions that occur in the five *skandhas* of form, feeling, thinking, activities, and consciousness. If one can contemplate and appreciate the various karmic retributions, one will fathom the nature of all dharmas without destroying it.

Wise people clearly understand all the Dharmas spoken by the Buddhas. Out of pity for beings, they cultivate the Bodhisattva conduct and dedicate all their accumulated good roots to them. Bodhisattvas see beings doing foolish things and so try to teach them, but beings are very deluded and do not understand.

Bodhisattvas teach beings to make sacrifices for the sake of others, to renounce the superficial aspects and seek the root of the matter, and to support and protect the Proper Dharma so that it will long abide in the world. But beings lack faith. That's why they are to be pitied. They should be exhorted to refrain from all evil and to practice all good. We should try to practice in accord with the true Dharma, constantly reflecting and asking ourselves: "Have we made mistakes in cause and effect? Instead of fulfilling our responsibilities within Buddhism, have we created all kinds of offenses?" We should constantly look within and examine ourselves again and again. Only then can we be considered genuine Buddhists.

TO BECOME A BUDDHA, STOP KARMA AND EMPTY EMOTIONS

Emotional attachments weigh us down. Psychological trauma often results.

WHEN SHAKYAMUNI Buddha left home to practice the Way, he was accompanied by three relatives from his father's side and two from his mother's side. In the end, however, these five people all left the Buddha. Why? Three of them found the Buddha's ascetic lifestyle too bitter, so they left the Buddha and took up other methods of practice. The other two saw the Buddha drink some porridge with milk and left in disgust, deciding that the Buddha was a weakling who couldn't take suffering. Which goes to show that it's impossible to please everyone.

> *The Buddhas and Bodhisattvas find it difficult,*
> *To fulfill the wishes of beings.*

Beings wish for different things. Their greed is insatiable. Once one wish is fulfilled, people start craving something else. Greed is insatiable, not unlike a bottomless pit. We have been greedy ever since the time we were born, from youth through our prime and into old age. Even at death we are still driven by greed. Those greedy for fame will die in the pursuit of fame. Those greedy for profit will die in the pursuit of profit. Pursuing fame, we will get burned to death; chasing after profit, we will die by drowning. Fame and profit bring down the disasters of water and fire. Pursue wealth and honor will die in the grips of the wind. Even so, everyone takes these mundane matters extremely seriously and cannot put them down.

When Shakyamuni Buddha was cultivating, he endured toil and suffering, but his fellow cultivators all abandoned him and went to follow other ways of practice. Now we are practicing according to Buddhism, and many people also disapprove of what we are doing. Fearing that they will lose out on things if they cultivate, they cannot muster any sincerity or make a true resolve.

Even after leaving the home-life to become monks or nuns, some people care only about getting their meals and don't do any work. Unconcerned about ending birth and death, they idly while away their time. When the ghost of impermanence comes for them, they'll have no control over their own birth and death. We will only be wasting our time if, after we leave home, we act like that. Anyone who thinks casually committing offenses is no problem should realize that to do so is to be a criminal within Buddhism.

While a prince, Shakyamuni Buddha cultivated extremely difficult ascetic practices and eventually became enlightened. After he became a Buddha, the first thing he did was to turn the Dharma Wheel of the Four Truths: suffering, accumulation, cessation, and the Way. As to suffering, there are the Three Sufferings, the Eight Sufferings, and limitless sufferings. The Three Sufferings are:

1. the suffering within suffering,
2. the suffering of decay, and
3. the suffering of process.

They are briefly described as follows:

1. The suffering within suffering is experienced by those who are so poor they don't even have a place to live, clothes to keep out the cold or heat, or food to eat. They suffer such extreme misery because they failed to cultivate in past lives. Instead, they cheated their teachers, scorned the teachings, engaged in evil, and were too clever and cunning for their own good. Not knowing enough to cultivate the Way, they fell and had to undergo suffering. Most of these people have just come from the animal realm. Because they slandered the Great Vehicle and cheated their teachers, they fell into the hells, underwent rebirth in the realms of hungry ghosts and animals, and finally became humans. Yet even as humans, their faculties are imperfect.

2. The suffering of decay. This type of suffering is undergone by those who are rich and honored. A person may have all he needs in terms of clothing, food, shelter, and transportation. He may own his own plane, boat, and mansion. But then a sudden fire burns up all his property, leaving him destitute. Or maybe he dies in a plane crash or a shipwreck. These belong to the suffering of decay. Everything had been going well, but then he loses everything, perhaps even his life. This is the suffering caused by the decay of blessings.

3. The suffering of process. Perhaps you are neither rich nor poor, and so you do not experience the previous two sufferings. You just lead a very ordinary life. From childhood, you enter the prime of life, grow old, and die. Your thoughts flow on in a continuous succession, and you cannot control them. When you grow old, your eyes get blurry, your ears become deaf, and your hands and feet are no longer nimble. This is the suffering of process.

The Three Sufferings hold tremendous sway over our lives. Even the greatest hero is sometimes overwhelmed by these sufferings, even to the point of dying. Isn't that pathetic?

Good deeds bring a good reward;
Evil deeds bring an evil retribution.

The retribution may come early or late, but we never fail to receive the blessings or calamities we deserve. We should take care not to commit limitless offenses in a moment of indulgence.

A single mistake brings everlasting regret;
By the time we recover, we will have reached a ripe old age.

No matter what happens, we have to maintain a righteous and proper spirit. After leaving the home-life, we should protect and practice the Proper Dharma. We must abide by the rules in every moment and not commit even the slightest transgression of the precepts. It is easy to create bad karma in a moment of carelessness. That's why there are said to be many Buddhist monks and Taoist priests at the gates of hell. Monks and nuns who don't follow the rules are headed for the hells. No mercy is shown to those who deliberately commit offenses. In fact, their punishment is tripled. It's not a lot of fun. Don't act recklessly, thinking that the Buddhas and Bodhisattvas cannot see you. Even the gods and spirits can read your mind, how much more the Buddhas and Bodhisattvas! Don't think you can do evil things because the Buddhas and Bodhisattvas have their eyes closed. You're just fooling yourself. Don't be like a thief who plugs up his ears while stealing a bell, hoping that others won't hear it. When it's time to suffer the consequences, it'll be too late to regret what you've done.

Lao Zi said, "I suffer great troubles because I have a body. Without a body, what troubles would I have?" People cannot relinquish their various attachments because they are locked in the cage of the five skandhas that comprise the body, the emotions, and the mind. Since they entertain various attachments, discriminations, and discursive thoughts, they cannot put an end to birth and death.

We also speak of the Eight Sufferings, although there are in fact infinite kinds of sufferings. The Eight Sufferings are:

1. the suffering of birth
2. the suffering of old age
3. the suffering of sickness
4. the suffering of death
5. the suffering of being apart from those you love
6. the suffering of being together with those you hate
7. the suffering of not obtaining what you want
8. the suffering of the raging blaze of the five *skandhas*

These Eight Sufferings are the most harmful things in the world. They are briefly explained below.

1. The suffering of birth. People have already suffered many hardships by the time they are born. When a mother eats cold food, the baby in her womb feels as if it's in the freezing mountains. When she eats hot food, the baby feels as if it's in a volcano. Being in the womb is an unpleasant experience. During birth, the baby cries because it feels as if it's being squeezed between two great mountains. The baby cries, "Ku! Ku! Ku!" ["Ku" means "suffering" in Chinese.] The baby is trying to say that it is in terrible pain, but it can't talk. If we didn't have bodies, we wouldn't feel pain and suffering. We experience all sorts of physical suffering through our bodies. Right at the time of birth, the baby's agony is like that of a live turtle whose shell is ripped off.

2. The suffering of old age. In old age, our eyes grow blurry, our ears become deaf, our teeth fall out, and our legs can't walk very well. We no longer have much control over our body. People can never truly feel at ease because of the tremendous afflictions caused by the first four sufferings of birth, old age, sickness and death.

3. The suffering of sickness. The human body is a false combination of the four elements: earth, air, fire, and water. Perhaps there is more fire than water, or more air than earth, or more water than fire. In general, if the four elements are not in balance, we become sick. We may suffer headaches, tender feet, sore arms, backaches, heart pain, sickness in the spleen or kidneys, and so on.

Each individual's sicknesses are different, and each sickness has its own cause. Lustful people tend to suffer kidney ailments. Greed for money can cause heart disease. A big temper makes the liver sick. Vexation and distress harm the lungs. Resentment causes spleen disease. Diseases of the heart, liver, spleen, lungs, and kidneys have their origin in hatred, resentment, affliction, anger, and vexation. Hating people harms the heart. Resenting people hurts the spleen. Getting afflicted at others hurts the lungs. Getting angry at others harms the liver. Too much distress harms the kidneys. When hatred, resentment, affliction, anger, and vexation act up, the four elements become unbalanced. An excess of joy, hate, sorrow, fear, or desire throws the four elements out of balance and causes various sicknesses. Sickness speeds up the aging process and brings on the suffering of old age.

4. The suffering of death. Birth leads inevitably to death. When a person dies, the four elements disperse and his spirit is dragged off by the karmic wind. Death entails unspeakable suffering.

5. The suffering of being apart from those you love. We are born as people in this evil world of the five turbidities because of love. If our emotional love were not so strong, we could be reborn in other worlds, such as the Land of Ultimate Bliss or the Lapis Lazuli Land. The ancients said,

> *If you didn't have such strong emotions,*
> *you wouldn't be born in the Saha World.*
> *If your karma is not emptied, you cannot be born in the*
> *Land of Ultimate Bliss.*

With karma ended and emotions emptied, one is a Buddha. With heavy karma and confused emotions, one is a common mortal. Worldly people are deluded by emotional love and cannot get beyond it. They think it's the best thing around. In reality, the stronger our passions, the more confused we become. Some people know very well that it's wrong, yet they want to get more deeply involved. As soon as boys and girls grow up, they are eager to get married and race down the same old road.

Love is a kind of emotional attachment that weighs us down. People experience psychological suffering and trauma because of love. When two people are in love, they are as if stuck together with glue; they need each other as much as fish need water. But if circumstances force them to separate, they experience the suffering of being apart from those they love; such partings are unbearably painful. These psychological ordeals are very hard to cope with.

6. The suffering of being together with those you hate. People who get along well can work together without conflict. But sometimes we may detest a person and want to get away from him. Yet no matter where we go, we keep meeting up with him. The more we hate him, the more we run into him. This is also a form of psychological suffering.

7. The suffering of not obtaining what you want. If you seek something, you are greedy for it. If you cannot obtain the object of your greed, you'll experience all sorts of afflictions. That's also a kind of suffering. Whether you desire fame, profit, wealth, or sex, if you cannot obtain it, you suffer. Even if you do obtain what you want, you won't be happy. Before obtaining it, you are anxious to get it. Once you've got it, you constantly worry about losing it. Your mind is never peaceful or happy. You always feel uneasy.

8. The suffering of the raging blaze of the five skandhas. The five *skandhas* are form, feeling, thinking, activities, and consciousness. It is very difficult for us to overcome them and see them as empty. The five *skandhas* burn us up and keep us in a state of agonizing pain.

The Eight Sufferings cause great vexation to human beings. But if you understand the way to mental and physical peace, these sufferings won't affect you.

The Eight Sufferings cannot disturb
The old monk who knows how to set himself at ease.

A talk given on May 1, 1982
at the City of Ten Thousand Buddhas

WHAT MEANING IS THERE TO LIFE?

If we do not wake up to our own birth and death, then, having been born muddled, we will also die muddled. What meaning is there to a life lived like that?

TIME FLIES, and the year has gone by before we know it. Next year is approaching. In the same way, people progress from birth to old age and death without being aware of it. Birth, old age, sickness, and death come in quick succession as we pass the years in muddled confusion. If we do not wake up to our own birth and death, then, having been born muddled, we will also die muddled. What meaning is there to this kind of life? Take a look! In every country and family, every person is taking this well-worn path of muddled birth and death; we lead our muddled lives in total ignorance.

How does ignorance come about? One unenlightened thought produces the three subtle attributes: the attribute of karma, the attribute of manifestation, and the attribute of turning. The three subtle attributes result in all the various differences in our lives. Each individual finds himself in various situations, and each has his own lot in life. Once we recognize what is going on, we should make a great resolve to reach enlightenment and seek wisdom and understanding. Since the Buddha has the greatest understanding and wisdom, he is called the Greatly Enlightened One. If we want to stop being muddled and attain understanding, we must first do our best to get rid of our bad habits and faults, for only then can our wisdom shine forth.

The lunar new year is coming, and I hope everyone will make a great resolve to seek enlightenment!

This day is already done, and our lives are that much less.
We're like fish in an ever-shrinking pond.
What joy is there in this?
Great assembly!
We should be diligent and vigorous, as if our own lives were at stake.
Only be mindful of impermanence, and be careful not to be lax.

A talk given on February 10, 1983
at the City of Ten Thousand Buddhas

CREATION NEVER STOPS; TRANSFORMATIONS NEVER CEASE

Desires for wealth, sex, fame, food, and sleep make people deluded. Traveling a dangerous road, they forget to return home. The more they wander, the farther they stray.

THE BUDDHA'S light can create living beings by transformation, and so it is said, "All living beings have the Buddha-nature, and all can become Buddhas."

As people, our breath can also generate an uncountable number of microorganisms. In the breath of one of these microorganisms, limitless numbers of other living beings also appear by transformation. However, while living beings transformed from the Buddha's spirit can become Buddhas as soon as they cultivate, the living beings who are transformed from those living beings are one level removed, so it isn't as easy for them to become Buddhas.

Animals can also create beings by transformation, because they have breath. A profusion of microorganisms is hidden in their breath. Under suitable conditions, they can turn into living beings. If the aiding conditions aren't present, they disappear. Similarly, there are infinite numbers of germs and bacteria in our bodies, which are also living beings. The germs can also create more germs by transformation.

If we analyze this more deeply, we find that large living beings can create large living beings by transformation, and small living beings can create small living beings by transformation. They are all multiplying prolifically, each within its own kind. Consequently, there are boundlessly many living beings in the world, and the more they multiply, the more numerous they become. When they multiply to the point that there isn't enough room in the world for so many living beings, the world will be destroyed. This world will be destroyed, and another world will be created. This is all part of the process of becoming deluded, creating karma, and undergoing retribution. Although we are deluded and muddled in this process, we don't try to gain a clear understanding, because we think we already understand very well.

The *Doctrine of the Mean* says, "People all say, 'I know,' but when they are driven into various nets, traps, or pitfalls, they don't know to escape." Would you call that wisdom or stupidity?

Living beings all need to eat. The reason whales can be trained to perform tricks obediently is that they want to eat. If they are rewarded with a piece of meat, they will do whatever they are told. People are controlled by their desires for wealth, sex, fame, food, and sleep; as a result they become deluded and muddled. They are traveling along a dangerous road and have forgotten to return home. The more they wander, the farther from home they stray. The farther they stray, the more they wander. Drifting and flowing in the bitter sea of birth and death, they don't know enough to pull themselves out. See how pitiful they are!

If living beings aren't confused by money, they're confused by sex.

They're always involved with these two things, and cannot get away from them. They may also be confused by food, by fame, or by sleep. These are all false attachments of living beings. They have no way to smash through their confusion. If they could, they would be free.

A talk given on August 29, 1982
at the City of Ten Thousand Buddhas

LIFE IS LIKE A DREAM: WAKE UP!

Where do we come from when we arrive? Where do we go to when we leave?

WHEN PEOPLE come into this world, they put down the real and pick up the unreal. That is why in life after life we turn against enlightenment, unite with the dust, and muddle our way through life as if drunk or in a dream. When we are born, we seem to be drunk and when we leave, we are unaware of how we die. People are all dreaming, and there's no knowing when they will wake up. It's said that life is like a dream. We take the false for the real, and become insatiably greedy for fame and profit.

In your dream, you are promoted and become wealthy; you have high social status, a good reputation, a beautiful wife, lovely mistresses, and a house full of children and grandchildren; you enjoy boundless affluence, wealth and honor.

If at some time during the dream someone were to tell you, "These things are all unreal," you would never believe that person. However, after you woke up from your sweet dream, even if no one told you it was a dream, you would know that you'd been dreaming.

Last night in a dream, you came out first in the imperial examinations, got appointed prime minister, later became emperor, and finally became an immortal enjoying boundless happiness. This morning you wake up. "Oh! It was a spring dream!" That is when you are awake. If you don't wake up and you continue to think it's real, then you become enamored of it and can't let go. Unable to let go, you become deeply attached and deluded. Right now we are daydreaming, not awake. So we come into this world muddled and leave muddled. Where do we come from when we arrive? Where do we go when we leave? We don't know. During our whole life long, we are never once awake. Think about it: Is that meaningful? What do we want to stay around for? What is so precious that we cannot bear to put it down?

In our lives, we are tightly bound by the ropes of the three poisons and the five desires. We don't even have the freedom to turn around, let alone be liberated. Hence, we must resolve to enter the monastic life and cultivate the Way, meditating and bowing to the Buddha with vigor. Those are the ways to untie the ropes of the three poisons and the five desires. The day will come when the ropes are completely untied. At that time, you will be awake. Looking back on what you have done, you will find that it was completely like a dream, and nothing you did was in accord with the Dharma. Since you now are fully awake, you can leave the Three Realms and not be bound by birth and death. You will have control over your own birth and death: you can be born if you like to and die when you want to. This state, where everything is just as you wish, where you can come and go freely, is true liberation. It is like waking up from a big dream.

But now we hold on to what's false and forget about what's true. What is false? The objects of the five desires: wealth, sex, fame, food and sleep. What is true? The happiness of the four virtues of Nirvana: eternity, bliss, true self, and purity. And yet we human beings are so strange: We're not afraid of losing what's true, but we're terrified when what's false is lost. Why is that? Because we take a thief for our son, we reject the roots in favor of the twigs, take the false for the true, and are continually dreaming, hooked by dream states.

Because of delusion, we create karma and then receive the retribution. We are like a dust mote floating up and down in the air, led by the power of our karma, revolving in the six paths, with no control of our own. It is said, "If you can't clear the hurdles of fame and profit, you won't be able to leap out of the cycle of rebirth." When fame and benefit cease to attract you, you'll escape the trap of rebirth in the six paths.

A talk given on August 21, 1983
at the City of Ten Thousand Buddhas

WHAT ARE WE LIVING FOR?

We should make it our top priority to benefit others. The first step in benefiting others is not to obstruct others.

WHAT ARE we living for? Who are we? What are we here for?

Someone says, “We’re here to collect garbage.” Is that so? Nowadays, people pick through things that others throw away, finding treasures in others’ garbage. People also plagiarize and copy others’ styles, while neglecting their own inherent talents. They rationalize, “If copying isn’t allowed, then where did other people get their styles from?” They renounce the essence and grasp at trivialities, making things worse by clumsily trying to imitate others. As a result, their own true wisdom remains concealed and undeveloped. The more they direct their attention outwards, the further away they drift! This is truly a great mistake.

But why are we born here? To pan gold and seek profit? No! To make fortunes? No! Money and material things are not truly useful. When the time comes to die, of what use are they?

What have we come into this world for? Since we have been born here, we should help the world and the people in it. Benefiting living beings is our duty. We shouldn't degrade the value of our life by directing it towards selfish ends. We should make benefiting others our top priority and always be concerned about humanity as a whole. The first step in benefiting others is not to obstruct others. To benefit ourselves at the expense of others, thus bringing harm and affliction to others, is not a proper thing to do.

Being born in this world, our first task is to establish merit and virtue; writing literature is secondary. Merit and virtue are invisible, while words are visible. It is said, "When words are cut off, the mind's activity ceases." If we arrive at that state, we are not far from enlightenment.

A talk given on the evening of March 21, 1980
at the City of Ten Thousand Buddha

THE IMPORTANCE OF CULTIVATION

Instead of thinking about how hard the Buddhas and Bodhisattvas work, we only know how to toil for our children

THE TRUE mind of living beings is no different from that of Buddhas. Why have the Buddhas accomplished proper enlightenment while living beings are still transmigrating in the six paths? Why are people still muddled and confused, obsessed with love all day long, unable to relinquish their attachments to their spouses and children? Why do beings remain continually caught up in the six kinds of sense perception?

Some people regard their families as far more important than studying Buddhism, and they always say, "I have my responsibilities." Well, when you die, who is going to take care of your responsibilities? Your attitude shows a confusion of priorities. If you realize that you should cultivate, just cultivate. Why have so many unnecessary concerns?

A Sutra says: "The Buddha, the World Honored One, has infinite spiritual power and wisdom." Spiritual power is itself wisdom.

Wisdom guides spiritual power. Spiritual power and wisdom are two, and yet not two. If you lack wisdom, you will not have spiritual power either. These come from the adornment of merit and virtue.

"Living beings have only infinite karmic bonds and afflictions." With careful reflection, we'll see that our various relationships with people are actually karmic entanglements. Having recklessly created karmic affinities in the past, we are now dragged about by our karma. We may want to escape the Triple Realm, but our karma will not let us. We have a mixture of good and bad karma, pure and defiled karma, karma of self and of others, and right and wrong karma, and it all comes forth. Hindered by our afflictions and caught up in birth and death, we pass our days in confusion.

Do you want to cultivate? "The time isn't right."

Would you like to cultivate? "I'll wait a few more years until the children have grown up."

"I'll wait a few more years until the children are married."

"I'll wait until I see my grandchildren."

"I'll wait until the grandchildren are married."

"I haven't seen my great grandchildren yet."

When will it ever end? Don't be taken in by the false happiness of the world. It is said,

Fame and benefit are trivial,
But everybody craves them.
Birth and death are important,
Yet no one guards againts them.

Many people worry that their children won't have money to spend, so they struggle to build an empire for them. The result:

When one has great wealth and property,
One's descendants will have great nerve:
Not afraid of anything under the sky,
They won't stop until they have destroyed
themselves and their families.

When one has little wealth and property,
One's descendants will not be so bold.
Petty problems are easily solved;
With modest assets, they will suffer few calamities.

The more money we leave to our children, the easier it is for them to bring great misfortunes upon themselves. The less money, the fewer the problems. It is also said,

If the son is more capable than the father,
What need is there to leave him wealth?
If the son is weaker than the father,
What's the use of leaving him money?

If your child is capable, why should you leave him money? If your child is weak, leaving him money only harms him, for he will use that money to eat, drink, be promiscuous, and gamble, generally leading a dissipated life.

"Although the nature of the mind is basically the same, delusion and enlightenment are as far apart as the sky and a deep abyss." Our minds are essentially the same as that of the Buddha. However, our delusion is worlds apart from the Buddha's enlightenment. "Quietly reflecting upon this, shouldn't we feel ashamed?" We are mindful of our sons and daughters, but not the Buddhas and Bodhisattvas. Instead of thinking about how hard the Buddhas and Bodhisattvas work, we only know how to toil for our children, sending them to universities so that they can earn doctorates and become super-achievers and high executives in the future. Then we will have chauffeured cars, gourmet food, fancy mansions, and all the luxury we could wish for.

"When you accomplish the cultivation of virtue, the virtue of your nature will manifest." When you have virtue in your cultivation, your inherent wisdom and spiritual power will spontaneously manifest. There is a saying:

Intelligence is aided by hidden virtue.
Hidden virtue brings about intelligence.
People who do not believe in hidden virtue
Will be hindered by their own intelligence.

Hidden virtue refers to acts of merit and virtue done anonymously-invisible good deeds. This means secretly helping others without taking credit for it.

A talk given on December 8, 1979

THE BODHI RESOLVE

Bringing forth the Bodhi resolve is like adding yeast to the dough, so that it will rise and expand over time.

WHAT is the Bodhi resolve? I have a very simple analogy: Before we make a committment to attain Bodhi, we are like flour before yeast is added. Bringing forth the Bodhi resolve is like adding yeast to the dough, so that it will rise and expand over time. What is the Bodhi resolve like? It is without any form or mark; it is none other than the enlightened Way. To be enlightened means to understand; to understand the principles of the Way. Yet we should not stop at understanding the principles; we must also cultivate the Way.

The Bodhi resolve can also be compared to a pagoda: no matter how tall a pagoda you plan to build, you have to start from the ground. The ground is analogous to our "mind ground." Just as we have to build a pagoda story by story from the ground up, the Bodhi resolve is similarly build up from the mind ground. Starting very small, it gradually grows greater and higher. And eventually, when we perfect our merit and virtue, we will become Buddhas.

BUSY DOING WHAT?

Rising early and retiring late, what keeps everyone so busy? Living beings are hard to save: it's pretty sad. Confused by the mundane world, they let their natures become upside-down. Even when reprimanded and given serious instruction, they still do not learn their lessons.

MOST people keep busy working all day. For what? For whom? In the last analysis, are we busy for our own sakes? Are we busy for someone else's sake? Are we busy for the sake of others? Most people would be hard put to answer these questions. Some might be flippant and say that we are "busy doing nothing."

Strange as in may seem, many people do things without really knowing why. Some people spend every waking moment intent upon their business, the point that they suffer perpetual insomnia. They are busy for the sake of money. The same thing happens to people who pursue scholarship, farming, laboring, and other livelihoods. If we want to succeed in any of those things, then we can't just do as we please. We must listen to our employer. We must get up early and retire late. As a passage from the *Book of Odes* says,

The cock has already crowed!
The morn is already upon us!

Oh! That's not that cock that crowed
It was just the buzzing of a fly.

That passage is describing a wise and virtuous emperor of old. As an emperor, he didn't sleep easily at night. The whole night long, he thought of nothing but the dawn, when he could get on with the day's business. In his anxiety for the night to pass, he rested so fitfully that he started at the sound of a buzzing fly and mistook it for the cock's crow. That is an instance of being busy for the sake of the people. It is said, "If there is a single man with blessings, the masses will put their trust in him." If there is a humane ruler who is worthy and intelligent, the populace will be able to put away their weapons, let their horses out to the pasture, and live in peace. However, the emperor himself must rise early and retire late, working for the prosperity of the people. How could he not do that?

We who cultivate the Way should also be busy from morning till night, not for the sake of profit, nor for the sake of fame, but for the sake of the Dharma. We should "serve the Buddhas without laxness from morning to night." We should get up early in the morning and go to bed late at night, and every day bow to the Buddhas and recite Sutras to display our devotion and sincerity as Buddhist disciples. It should not be that we say the right things but our hearts are false. It should not be that we can talk but not practice.

When we bow to the Buddhas, we should concentrate single-mindedly and show respect with our bodies. Bowing to the Buddhas can eradicate obstacles created by our offenses. It is said, "To bow before the Buddhas can eradicate offenses as numerous as the grains of sand in the Ganges." It is a good thing offenses are formless. If they were solid objects they would fill up worlds as numerous as the Ganges' sands. Therefore, from morning till night, we should bow to the Buddhas and recite the Buddhas' names to eradicate obstacles created by our offenses. We should be busy for the sake of the Dharma.

But living beings' dispositions are hard to fathom. For instance, if they like to eat sweets and you give them something sour, they will be unhappy. But on the other hand, if you give sweet things to people who like to eat sour things, then they get upset. That's the way they all are. If you don't understand each individual's disposition, you will have no way to save people. Only the Buddha's wisdom is sufficient to be familiar with living beings' basic natures, and because of that, the Buddha can offer teaching that is appropriate to each one. He is constantly on the move, roaming about, accepting toil and suffering in order to save living beings. But even that doesn't please living beings. They still will not accept the teachings of the Buddhas and Bodhisattvas. "Living beings are hard to save: it's pretty sad." "Sad" means deep regret to the point of grief. Because living beings are so foolish and end up so upside-down, the Buddhas and Bodhisattvas constantly use great compassion on their behalf.

Why are living beings so hard to save? "Confused by the mundane world, they let their natures become upside-down." That's one answer. Throughout limitless eons, living beings have become deeply tainted by the defiling six sense objects. They continually thrash around in the sea of suffering, surfacing and sinking. They take suffering for bliss and the false for the true. Thus people of today become so caught up in "fashion," that even when the current styles are unattractive and may lead to undesirable consequences, they still compete to stay in fashion. People don't know that the sea of suffering is boundless, but a turn of the head is the other shore. Take military weapons for instance: not only do people fail to get rid of them, they seek to improve their arsenals. Great effort is exerted in inventing new weapons of mass destruction, which become more and more lethal. If that isn't upside-down, what is?

Sages and wise advisors earnestly admonish us, repeating their exhortations over and over in order to guide us pitiful creatures. They are like elders who discipline their children. But living beings ignore those messages as if they hadn't even heard them, to the point that they employ thousands of methods and hundreds of schemes to hide away their offenses so their teachers and elders won't find out about them. "Even when reprimanded and given serious instruction, they still do not learn their lessons."

Ah! The talent living beings have for committing offenses is truly endless! The Buddhas and Bodhisattvas find it hard to save us pitiful creatures. What a sad situation!

A talk given on the morning of June 16, 1958

OUTFLOWS GONE, WISDOM SHINES

Thoughts of desire will plunder our treasures. They are worse than a gang of bandits.

ALL THE Buddhas, Bodhisattvas, Worthy Ones and Sages of the All Buddhas, Bodhisattvas, sages, and worthy ones of the Sangha can emit the unsurpassed light of wisdom. Their wisdom is free of outflows and therefore, never-ending.

People have outflows because they have ignorance. Buddhas and Bodhisattvas have no outflows because they have no ignorance. Being ignorant means not understanding things. It means being muddled, unable to tell right from wrong, or black from white.

The biggest outflow is the outflow of desire. Thoughts of desire will plunder our treasures. They are worse than a gang of bandits. They render us useless, like wood infested with termites. They poison us, like delicious food tainted with manure. Someone says, "But everyone has thoughts of desire!" That's exactly the reason we must cultivate. We have to get rid of thoughts of desire before our inherent wisdom can come forth. Eliminating outflows is the extraordinary state sought by cultivators.

Everyone should pay close attention. Why is the spiritual power of Elimination of Outflows one of the six spiritual powers? Elimination of Outflows means being totally free of desire. Desire is cut off; emotional love ceases to function. If we can cultivate until we attain mastery, we will experience a sense of freedom and ease. If people don't put an end to love and desire, but are always controlled by ignorance, they will do upside-down things and be ill at ease all day long, because those thoughts of desire will keep them stirred up.

All Good and Wise Advisors! You should especially apply effort in this, return to the source, recover your original face—at that point, you will attain an inexhaustible wisdom which comes forth incessantly. No matter how much you use, it will never be exhausted. Each of you must bring forth the resolve for Bodhi—only then can you smash through the gate of birth and death. You must look within yourself and ask your conscience: Why do I believe in the Buddha? Why did I chose monastic life? Why don't I cultivate now that I'm a monk? Having left home, why do I still have so many idle thoughts? Don't ignore these questions. You should think them through clearly! Then you'll be able to leave the Triple Realm, end birth and death, and attain the bliss of Nirvana.

THE TEN DHARMA REALMS

Where do the Ten Dharma Realms come from?

If anyone wishes to understand
All people of the three periods of time,
He should contemplate the nature of the
Dharma Realm;
The Tathagatas are made from the mind
alone.

IF ANYONE *wishes to understand.* Suppose there are people who wish to understand how people become people.

All people of the three periods of time. "Shouldn't it be 'all Buddhas of the three periods of time'? Why did you say 'all people of the three periods of time'?" you ask. People are Buddhas. If you call a person a Buddha, that's okay; and if you call the Buddha a person, that's okay, too. Why is this? Because a person can become a Buddha. A Buddha is just a person who has realized Buddhahood. If you talk about Buddhas, no one really understands. "What's a Buddha?" they ask. Everyone knows what a person is. So we'll talk about people, and it will become easier to understand.

Who are the people we're discussing? The Buddhas.

"Am I a Buddha?" you ask.

You are.

"Are other people Buddhas?"

Yes, they are too. You are a Buddha, but an unrealized Buddha. After your realization, you will become a true Buddha. Now you are a false Buddha. False Buddhas can become true Buddhas, and true Buddhas can become false Buddhas. If anyone wishes to understand / All Buddhas of the three periods of time. The verse starts with the word "if" to indicate that this is only a hypothetical situation; don't be attached and think that it's real. The Buddhas of the three periods of time are just people who have realized Buddhahood.

He should contemplate the nature of the Dharma Realm. How can the Dharma Realm have a nature? If it had a nature, how could it be called the Dharma Realm? Actually, this refers to the nature of the living beings in the Dharma Realm. Every living being of the Dharma Realm has its own nature. You have your nature, and I have my nature. "I don't know what you mean by 'nature'." You say. Well, your temper is bigger than mine; and mine is deeper than yours. Thus, our natures are different.

Each living being in the Dharma Realm has its own nature. Pigs have the nature of pigs; horses have the nature of horses. Men have the nature of men, and women have the nature of women. Each has his or her own nature. Those who like to eat sweet things have a sweet nature; those who like to eat sour things have a sour nature; those who like hot, spicy things have a hot nature. Those who like to eat bitter things have a bitter nature, like all of us here. [Note: In Chinese, the same character means both 'bitter' and 'ascetic.'] We cultivate ascetic practices.

Cultivation is ascetic practice; even going to the dining hall to eat is an ascetic practice. When it comes to ascetic practices, none of you should fall behind. You should race toward the front. In the "ascetic practice" of eating, all of you race toward the front, don't you?

If you look into it, you'll find that everything has its own nature. Trees have the nature of trees; flowers have the nature of flowers; grass has the nature of grass. Each thing has its own nature. So "the nature of the Dharma Realm" refers to the nature of each living being in the Dharma Realm. Do you understand? Previously you thought that the Dharma Realm had a nature, but now you know this is referring to the nature of living beings in the Dharma Realm.

The Tathagatas are made from the mind alone. The original verse from the *Avatamsaka Sutra* said: If anyone wishes to understand / All Buddhas of the three periods of time, / He should contemplate the nature of the Dharma Realm; / Everything is made from the mind alone. I changed the second line to say, All people of the three periods of time, and I also changed the last line to The Tathagatas are made from the mind alone. Buddhas are created from the mind. If your mind cultivates the Buddhadharma, you will become a Buddha. If your mind likes the Bodhisattvas, you can practice the Bodhisattva Way and become a Bodhisattva. If your mind wants to fall into the hells, you are bound to fall.

1) The Dharma Realm of Buddhas

Neither great nor small,
Neither gone nor come,
In worlds as many as motes of dust,
They shine upon each other from their lotus thrones.

The first Dharma Realm is that of Buddhas. I once gave a lecture in Redwood City (California) in which I explained the word "Buddha." Because I'm quite dull and a bit deaf, when I first heard the word "Buddha" in English, I heard it as *bu da*, which means "not big" in Chinese. What is "not big"? The Buddha. One professor liked my explanation so much that when I finished my lecture, he put his palms together and said to me, *"Bu da."*

"Not big" means not arrogant. The Buddha is not arrogant or haughty. An arrogant person is someone who is always saying, "I! I! I!" The Buddha doesn't have an "I," an ego. "Me, me, me"—everything is "me." Everything to the right, left, in front, back, above, below, and throughout the four directions is "me." There are too many "me's," and so the self becomes big. The Buddha, being selfless, is "not big." Then is he little? No. If he were little, he wouldn't be a Buddha. He is *neither great nor small.*

Neither gone nor come. The Buddha has "come and yet not come, gone and yet not gone." Since the Buddha's Dharma-body fills all of space and pervades the Dharma Realm, it is neither absent nor present. You may speak of the Buddha as going, but to where does he go? You might say he comes, but from where does he come? Nor does his Dharma-body merely pervade our world; the Dharma Realm includes as many worlds as there are motes of dust—limitlessly, boundlessly many worlds—all of which are the Buddha's Dharma-body.

In worlds as many as motes of dust. They shine upon each other from their lotus thrones. The Buddha in this Dharma Realm shines his light upon the Buddha of another Dharma Realm, and the light of the Buddha in that Dharma Realm illumines this Dharma Realm. Sitting on lotus thrones, the Buddhas simultaneously move the earth and emit light from their ears, eyes, noses, tongues, and teeth. Not only do their six organs put forth light and move the earth, their every pore emits light and moves the earth. And in every pore, worlds as numerous as motes of dust appear, each containing incalculable numbers of Buddhas who emit light in the same way.

Yet all these lights, like those of many lamps, do not contend. One lamp doesn't say to another, "You can't give off so much light, because my light has nowhere to go." The lights don't clash with one another; they fuse together. In Buddhism, we unite our lights. Just as lights do not conflict with one another, so too should people not clash. We should allow our lights to shine on one another like the lights interpenetrating at the interstices of the infinitely-layered circular net canopy of the Great Brahma Heaven King. That's the Dharma Realm of Buddhas.

2) The Dharma Realm of Bodhisattvas

> *Sentient beings when enlightened*
> *Leap out of the dust.*
> *Their six perfections and ten thousand practices*
> *At all times are nurtured.*

The second Dharma Realm is that of Bodhisattvas. Why did I say All people of the three periods of time above? It's because people can cultivate to go to any of the Ten Dharma Realms. Yet people are not beyond a single thought of the mind.

The Sanskrit word Bodhisattva is translated as "enlightened being" and has two meanings:

1. one who causes all sentient beings to become enlightened
2. an enlightened one among all sentient beings

We are included in both meanings. We all have a share of Bodhisattvahood because we are all beings. We can become enlightened ones among beings, and we can teach other beings to become enlightened as well. So being a Bodhisattva isn't bad. Not only do we have a share of Bodhisattvahood, we also have a share of Buddhahood.

"I don't get it," you say. "Dharma Master, you said earlier that Buddhas are just people who have realized Buddhahood. Well, why haven't we become Buddhas?"

Let's not talk about people becoming Buddhas. Consider a small child who grows up, becomes an adult, and eventually gets old. We are like children within the Buddhadharma, and the Buddha is an adult. When we grow up, we will become Buddhas. But right now, we are still children in Buddhism. As youngsters need milk, we constantly need the nourishment of hearing the Dharma. Listening to the Dharma is an especially good way to make our good roots grow and to bring forth our wisdom. An opportunity to listen to the Dharma is more valuable than any amount of money you could earn.

Today I'm going to make a rule. I hope that from now on all of you will not take so many holidays and go on so many trips. Take the study of the Buddhadharma as your trip. Spend your holidays studying the Buddhadharma. Why do I say this? Because it's very dangerous to travel. Every holiday there are many fatalities, and if you travel, you might end up being one of them. We want to change the trends of this country. The people in this country are fond of recreation and travel. Buddhists should not take so many vacations. We can use this time to study the Buddhadharma. Even better, we can chant sutras, recite mantras, and bow to the Buddhas!

There is infinite merit and virtue in bowing to the Buddhas.

Bowing before the Buddhas can eradicate offenses
As numerous as the Ganges' sands.

If you bow to the Buddhas, you can cancel as many offenses as there are grains of sand in the Ganges River. It is also said, "Giving a single penny brings limitless blessings." However, I'm certainly not asking for money from you. You should understand that. You can make contributions to other monasteries and earn great blessings that way. We here are so wretched that we don't have the blessings to receive offerings. If we accept too many offerings, we might die. If no one makes offerings, maybe we can live a few days more. Despite the suffering, we still wish to live a little longer. We don't want to die yet. Therefore, if you wish to give money, you can give it to other places. There are plenty of places where you can plant blessings; you don't have to do it at this monastery, because Gold Mountain Monastery has only wretched people with few blessings. If you seek blessings here, you'll be disappointed. But don't worry, we won't starve!

Sentient beings when enlightened. Leap out of the dust. Their six perfections and ten thousand practices.

At all times are nurtured. A Bodhisattva is a sentient being; among sentient beings, he's an enlightened one. Among the enlightened, he's one who understands. Among those who understand, he's a cultivator. Among cultivators, he's one who truly practices. A Bodhisattva "leaps out of the dust." If he did not have understanding, he wouldn't be able to transcend the defilement. The dust would be so thick that he wouldn't be able to leap out of it. When he becomes enlightened, the dust thins out and he can leap out of it.

"After a Bodhisattva leaps out of the dust, what does he do? Sleep and eat?"

Yes, he still sleeps, eats, and wears clothes; but he no longer works like a slave to provide his body with food, clothing, and a place to live. When you get out of the dust, you cease to be concerned with these three problems, and instead you concentrate on cultivating the six perfections: giving, holding precepts, patience, vigor, concentration, and wisdom.

"I know what the perfection of giving entails. It involves telling others to make offerings to me," some of you are thinking. Wrong. It is learning to give to other people. As for money, it would be nice to shred it up. We shouldn't want so much of that filthy stuff. Money is an extremely defiling possession, and too much involvement with it is what is meant by "dust." If you don't want money, then you will be extremely pure and will be able to transcend the "dust." Some of you have now transcended the "dust" because you are holding the precept of not handling money. However, make sure you don't get contaminated by money again in the future.

You should also cultivate the ten thousand practices and nurture them at all times. You cannot say, "I'll cultivate today, but not tomorrow. I'll cultivate this year, but not next year. I'll cultivate this month and take a rest next month. I'll cultivate this life, but not next life." To cultivate one moment and sleep the next moment won't work. At all times you should nurture your cultivation of the six perfections and ten thousand practices. Cultivate them in life after life. If you practice in this way, you will be a Bodhisattva.

"That's not easy," you say.

Did you think that being a Bodhisattva would be easy? Not only is it not easy to be a Bodhisattva, it's not easy to be a Shravaka or a Pratyekabuddha, either.

"Then what is it easy to be?"

It is easy to be a ghost, to go to the hells, or to become an animal. If you want things to be easy, you can be those beings. If you want to be a Bodhisattva, it won't be easy. You say it's difficult; the word "difficult" describes what Bodhisattvas do.

Bodhisattvas must be able to do what others cannot do; they must endure what others find difficult to endure. When people consider a job too difficult, they say, "That's all right; we'll handle it." They are not put off by difficult tasks. If you don't dare to do what is hard, you are not a Bodhisattva. Go forth with vigor! That's what a Bodhisattva is like; there is no other esoteric or wonderful secret. If you can do the things that other people cannot do, you are a Bodhisattva.

3) The Dharma Realm of Those Enlightened to Conditions

The holy sages enlightened to conditions
Doze high on mountain peaks alone.
Springtime's flowers wither in the fall
In a cycle of twelve interconnecting links.

Why am I asking you all these questions? Those Enlightened to Conditions (Pratyekabuddhas) don't like questions. They are recluses who don't like to be around other people. Today we are looking into the question of everyone being together, so you should not act like Those Enlightened to Conditions. When there is a Buddha in the world, they are called Those Enlightened to Conditions. When there is no Buddha in the world, they are called Solitarily Enlightened Ones, because they are able to become enlightened by themselves.

What do they like to do? They like to sleep in solitude on the mountain peaks. *The holy sages enlightened to conditions. / Doze high on mountain peaks alone. / Springtime's flowers wither in the fall. / In a cycle of twelve interconnecting links.* Speaking of Those Enlightened to Conditions, we should also become enlightened to causes and conditions. They cultivate the twelve causes and conditions. We, however, are cultivated by the twelve causes and conditions.

The first of the twelve causes and conditions is *ignorance.* They contemplate ignorance. "Where does it comes from? Strange! How can there be ignorance?" Then they see that ignorance leads to activity.

With the manifestation of *activity,* consciousness appears. *Consciousness* involves discrimination. Activity is a conditioned dharma while ignorance is neither conditioned nor unconditioned; it is between the two.

Why are discriminations made? Because of conditioned dharmas. The discriminating mind is a result of conditioned dharmas. With a discriminating mind, the trouble starts. *Name and form* are the trouble. "Name" brings the trouble of name, and "form" brings the trouble of form. If I didn't talk about them, there wouldn't be any problems. Just mentioning them is asking for trouble, because you're bound to say, "How are name and form troublesome? I don't understand." Now you have the added trouble of "not understanding." Before I said anything, you didn't have that problem. Once I began talking, the problem of your not understanding arose and with it came the desire to know.

This quest for knowledge results in the use of the *six sense faculties.* See? The six sense faculties come into being because of the wish to understand. Have you ever heard such an explanation? No one has explained it this way before.

When you decide you want to know, the eyes, ears, nose, tongue, body, and mind appear. You think you can gain understanding through them without realizing that the more you want to understand, the more confused you become, and the more confused you are, the less you understand.

Since you do not understand, you seek *contact.* You go around making contact at random: east, west, south, north, above, below; like a fly madly bouncing off the walls. Why does it bounce off the walls? Because it wants to understand.

Contact is just bumping up against things, going everywhere bouncing off the walls. You go everywhere hoping to understand, but all that results from this desperate attempt is a lot of bruises. After the determination to understand sets in and encounters occur, there is *feeling.* "Ow, that hurts!" Or, "Ah, I'm so comfortable. Right now I'm not bumping into things, and I feel really good." But when you bump against something, you don't feel good at all. You feel happy if no one is telling you that you're not nice. But you get upset when you hear someone criticize you. This is where feeling lies; it cannot be found outside.

Once there is feeling, craving and attachment arise. You give rise to craving and attachment for pleasant situations, but you feel aversion for unpleasant environments. Happiness and unhappiness come from craving and aversion, and so every day the trouble grows.

The holy sages enlightened to conditions. Doze high on mountain peaks alone. Springtime's flowers wither in the fall. In a cycle of twelve interconnecting links. The myriad things grow and prosper in the springtime, so the Pratyekabuddha sages contemplate and realize that everything undergoes the natural process of birth and death. They "contemplate the hundreds of flowers blossoming in the springtime, and watch the dry leaves falling in the autumn." They contemplate the twelve causes and conditions.

Now we come to craving. The reason people feel unsettled is because of craving. Once there is craving, there is also aversion. You grasp at those things that you crave. What is meant by *grasping?* It means wanting to get hold of something. Because you have craving, you then want to obtain those objects in order to fulfill your desires. Thus grasping leads to becoming. Once you have these things for your own, there is further *birth,* which leads to *old age and death.* These are the twelve causes and conditions cultivated by Those Enlightened to Conditions.

4) The Dharma Realm of Hearers

The Shravaka disciples,
Both men and women,
Contemplate and practice the Four Noble Truths,
Concealing the real and displaying the expedient.

There are Hearers (Shravakas) of the first fruition, the second fruition, the third fruition, and the fourth fruition. This Dharma Realm is further divided into (a) those approaching the first fruition, who have not yet realized the fruition; (b) those who have realized first fruition; (c) those approaching the second fruition; (d) those who have realized the second fruition; (e) those approaching the third fruition; (f) those who have realized the third fruition; (g) those approaching the fourth fruition; and (h) those who have realized the fourth fruition.

Hearers are also called Arhats. Arhats can fly and transform themselves, and they possess supernatural powers. One should not casually claim that he has attained the fruition, saying, "I'm an Arhat." That is not allowed. When a sage who has attained the fruition walks, his feet do not touch the ground. Although he appears to be walking on the road, he is actually traveling in the air. His feet do not touch the ground or the dirt. Even if he walks across mud, his shoes remain clean. Dharma Master Du Shun [the first patriarch of the Huayan School], for example, was one whose shoes weren't soiled when he walked over mud. This is the sign of a sage who has attained the fruition. One cannot casually claim to have attained the fruition.

Hearers of the first fruition have eliminated view delusions. Those of the second fruition eliminate thought delusions. At the level of the third fruition, they eliminate delusions in number like dust and sand. The Hearer of the fourth fruition has partially, though not completely, eliminated ignorance. Only one who has completely destroyed ignorance realizes Buddhahood, for even a Bodhisattva at the stage of equal enlightenment still has a small amount of the ignorance of arising phenomena which keeps him from realizing Buddhahood. What Dharmas do sages of the fourth fruition cultivate? Everyone knows the Dharmas they cultivate; we've all heard them before. They are: suffering, the cause of suffering, the cessation of suffering, and the Way to the cessation of suffering.

In the beginning, Shakyamuni Buddha went to the Deer Park to teach those people who were to become the first five Bhikshus. This included the Venerable Ajnatakaundinya and the Venerable Ashvajit. These five people were, in fact, relatives of the Buddha. They had followed the Buddha to practice, but some of them couldn't endure the hardship. When Shakyamuni Buddha was cultivating in the Himalayas, he became as thin as a stick, because he ate only one sesame seed and one grain of wheat each day. Three of his followers found this unbearable and fled in hunger, and only two remained. Later, on the eighth day of the twelfth lunar month, a heavenly maiden offered some milk to Shakyamuni Buddha, and he accepted it. At that point, the other two followers left as well, not because they couldn't stand the hardship, but because they felt that the Buddha didn't know how to practice. They said, "You're supposed to be cultivating ascetic practices, and yet you drank milk. That shows you aren't able to cultivate and endure hardship." Therefore, they left as well. All five of them went to the Deer Park.

After Shakyamuni became a Buddha, he first spoke the *Avatamsaka Sutra,* which very few beings were able to understand. He then "concealled the true and offered the expedient teaching," and he spoke the *Agama Sutras.* "Whom should I teach?" the Buddha wondered. Then he recalled, "Previously I had five fellow cultivators who supported my practice. I should teach them first, because in the past I vowed that when I became a Buddha, I would first teach those who have slandered me, killed me, or treated me badly." Who had treated the Buddha the worst? If you've read the *Vajra Sutra,* you'll know about King Kali. At the level of planting causes, when Shakyamuni Buddha was cultivating as a patient immortal, King Kali had chopped off the limbs of his body. Why?

In that previous life, Shakyamuni Buddha was a skilled cultivator. His body was covered with a thick layer of dust and dirt, and he never went down the mountain. He remained there cultivating ascetic practices. One day King Kali took his concubines—his wives—along on a deer hunt. The women accompanied him into the mountains, but had no interest in hunting with the King. They wanted to have fun on their own. While strolling around in the mountains, they came upon a strange creature…they weren't quite sure what it was. Its eyebrows were three inches long and its hair was two feet long. Its face seemed to have never been washed, for the dirt caked on it was extremely thick. The dirt on its clothing was at least an inch thick.

When these women saw it, they couldn't figure out what it was. They said, "It's a monster! Let's get out of here!"

Then the cultivator said, "You don't have to leave; I'm not a monster."

"It can speak!" they gasped. One of the braver ones asked him, "What are you doing here?"

He replied, "I'm cultivating."

She asked, "What do you mean by 'cultivating'?"

He said, "I'm cultivating in order to become a Buddha." Then he taught them the Dharma.

The women grew friendlier and expressed their concern, "You endure so much difficulty here. What do you eat?"

He answered, "I eat whatever there is—roots and leaves. I don't go out asking for food from people." By that time the women's fears vanished. One of them reached out to touch his eyebrows; another touched his hands, and yet a third patted his face. They viewed the cultivator as something precious and tried to get closer to him.

Meanwhile, King Kali had finished hunting and was looking for his concubines. He found them all gathered around something and tried to see what they were up to. He walked his way slowly toward them, not making a sound, and when he was close enough he saw them talking with a very strange man. What is more, one was touching his hands and another was patting his feet! Seeing them acting so friendly, the King immediately grew jealous. The cultivator was talking to his women about cultivation.

In a rage, the King bellowed, "You have no business cheating my women! What are you cultivating?"

The cultivator replied, "I'm cultivating patience."

"And what do you mean by 'patience'?"

"I will not become angry at anyone who scolds or beats me."

King Kali said, "You may have cheated my women into believing you, but I'll never believe you. You say you can be patient? Is that true?"

The old cultivator said, "Of course."

"Fine, I'm going to give you a test!" The King then drew his sword and chopped off the old cultivator's hand. He said, "I've just chopped off your hand. Do you hate me?"

The cultivator said, "No."

"You don't hate me? Then you really have some skill. But you must be lying. You just say you don't hate me, even though in your mind you do. You're lying! I'm a very smart person. You think you can fool me?" King Kali continued, "All right, since you claim you are patient and don't hate me, I'm going to chop off your other hand."

After chopping off the cultivator's other hand, the King asked, "Now do you hate me?"

The old cultivator said, "No."

The King then chopped off the cultivator's feet. Having hacked off the cultivator's four limbs, he asked, "Do you hate me?"

"No," said the cultivator, "not only do I not hate you, but when I accomplish Buddhahood, I will save you first. How can I convince you that I don't hate you? If I hate you, my four limbs will not be restored, and if I don't hate you, my hands and feet will be restored, even though you have completely severed them from my body. If they are restored, that will prove that I don't feel any hatred. If I feel any hatred, that will not occur." Whereupon the old cultivator became whole again.

Having witnessed King Kali hack off the cultivator's hands and feet in such a cruel manner, the Dharma-protecting spirits manifested their great supernatural power and pelted the King with a shower of hailstones. Realizing the severity of his offense and seeing the cultivator's great spiritual powers, King Kali knelt before the cultivator seeking forgiveness.

The cultivator said, "If I don't realize Buddhahood, there is nothing to be said. But if one day I do, I will save you first." That is why the Buddha first went to the Deer Park to teach Ajnatakaundinya, who had been King Kali in a former life. Because of his past vow, the Buddha first wanted to save the person who had treated him the worst.

After hearing this story, we should all vow that after becoming Buddhas, we will first save those who treated us the worst. We shouldn't think, "You've been so mean to me. I'm going to send you to the hells after I become a Buddha." Don't make that kind of vow.

When the Buddha went to the Deer Park, he spoke the three turnings of the Dharma Wheel of the Four Noble Truths for the five Bhikshus. First he said:

> This is suffering; it is oppressive.
>
> This is the cause of suffering; it beckons.
>
> This is the Way; it can be cultivated.
>
> This is the cessation of suffering; it can be realized.

The second time he said,

> This is suffering; I have completely known it.
>
> This is the cause of suffering; I have completely eliminated it.

This is the Way; I have completely cultivated it.

This is the cessation of suffering; I have completely realized it.

During the third turning he said,

This is suffering; you should know it.

This is the cause of suffering; you should eliminate it.

This is the Way; you should cultivate it.

This is the cessation of suffering; you should realize it.

After the Buddha spoke the three turnings of Four Noble Truths, he said to Ajnatakaundinya, "You are troubled by guest-dust [transient defilements] and have not obtained liberation."

When Ajnatakaundinya heard the words "guest-dust," he became enlightened and realized the transience of defiling objects. "The guest is not the host, and the dust is unclean. My self-nature is the host, and it is clean and pure." Ajnatakaundinya is called "one who understands the original limit." He understood the fundamental truth and became the "foremost exponent of emptiness."

The Four Noble Truths are infinite and inexhaustible. *The Shravaka disciples, / Both men and women.* Both women and men can realize the fruition and become Hearers, or Arhats. Dharma Master Kumarajiva's mother, for instance, became a third-stage Arhat.

Hearers *contemplate and practice the Four Noble Truths.* They cultivate the Four Noble Truths: suffering, the cause of suffering, the cessation of suffering, and the Way. This involves being aware of suffering, eliminating the cause of suffering, aiming for the cessation of suffering, and cultivating the Way. They cultivate the Dharma-door of the Four Noble Truths.

Concealing the real and displaying the expedient. You see them as

Hearers, but in reality they may be great Bodhisattvas of the provisional teaching who appear expediently as such. This is called "concealing the real." They conceal their real merit and virtue. "Displaying the expedient" means they demonstrate skillful means. Hearers may be great Bodhisattvas who have come back to the world. Not all of them are, but some of them are definitely Great Vehicle Bodhisattvas who appear among those of the Theravada to urge them to progress toward the great. This is called "concealing the real and displaying the expedient."

5) The Dharma Realm of Gods

Beings of the Six Desire and the Brahma heavens,
Practice the five precepts and the ten good deeds.
Planting seeds with outflows,
They cannot terminate their transmigration.

Beings of the Six Desire and the Brahma Heavens. First of all, there are the Six Desire Heavens, which are the Heavens of the Desire Realm. There are heavens in the Desire Realm, the Form Realm, and the Formless Realm—in all of the Three Realms.

Our world is located under the first of the six heavens of the Desire Realm—the Heaven of the Four Heavenly Kings. This heaven, which is directly above us, is governed by the four Heavenly Kings. It is located halfway up Mount Sumeru, which means that half of Mount Sumeru is within the human realm while the other half is above the Heaven of the Four Heavenly Kings. The parts of this heaven located on the north, south, east, and west sides of Mount Sumeru are governed by the four Heavenly Kings, as are the four continents of our world: Purvavideha to the east, Jambudvipa to the south, Aparagodaniya to the west, and Uttarakuru to the north. If we were to go into detail, we would never finish our discussion of this heaven.

The beings in the Heaven of the Four Heavenly Kings have a life span of 500 years, but that's not the same as 500 years in our world. One day and night in that heaven is equal to 50 years on earth. Figure it out: How many years on earth is 500 years in the Heaven of the Four Heavenly Kings? The beings in that heaven live for 500 years. One of their days is 50 human years. How many human years is 365 of their days? If you know math, you can figure it out.

The second heaven in the Desire Realm is the Trayastrimsha Heaven. Trayastrimsha (Trayastri) is a Sanskrit word. You don't know what that means? Then let's call it the "Don't Know Heaven." The Don't Know Heaven is just the Trayastrimsha, a Sanskrit word that means "thirty-three." *Shakra,* known as **yin tuo la ye** (Indra) in the Shurangama Mantra, resides in the center of these heavens. He is the "God" revered in Christianity, and in China he is known as the Jade Emperor. The Book of History (Shu-jing) refers to him as the Supreme Lord and says, "Bathe and observe purity in order to worship the Supreme Lord."

In ancient China no one knew about the Buddha; they knew only about the Supreme Lord. In the Shang Dynasty, Emperor Tang used a black bull as an offering to the Supreme Lord and said, "I, Lü, but a small child, presume to use this black bull in venturing to make known to the Supremely Exalted Ruling Lord that if I have offenses, they are not the people's, and if the people have offenses, the offenses rest with me."

Emperor Tang's name was Lü, and he referred to himself as a small child out of respect for the Supreme Lord. He very sincerely offered a black bull and told the Supreme Lord that if he made errors, the citizens should not be blamed, and that if the common folk of his country committed offenses, the responsibility should rest with the Emperor for not having taught them correctly.

The ancients blamed themselves in that way, unlike people of today who clearly know that they are in the wrong but say, "Don't look at me! It's his fault! How can you blame me?" and complain, "God is unjust.

Why does he confer wealth on others and make me so poor? Why does he bestow honor on some and leave me so wretched?" They blame heaven and curse mankind, looking for faults in others instead of admitting their own wrongs. The ancients acknowledged their own mistakes.

In the Trayastrimsha Heaven, Shakra resides in the middle, with eight heavens surrounding him to the north, south, east, and west, making thirty-three in all.

The third of the Desire Heavens is the Yama [Suyama] Heaven. Yama is a Sanskrit word which means "time period." In this heaven, the gods are so happy that they sing songs about their bliss day and night. They sing, "How happy I am! I'm so happy!" They are joyful throughout the six periods of the day and night. Hence, the name of this heaven is translated as "time period." Every time period is filled with happiness.

The fourth of the Desire Heavens is the Tushita Heaven, which translates as "happiness and contentment." The beings there are always happy and satisfied. Those who know contentment are always happy. That heaven is also called the "Heaven of Contentment," because the beings there never have a worry or care from morning to night. They don't have any afflictions or worries.

The fifth of the Desire Heavens is the Heaven of the Transformation of Bliss (Nirmalarati). The beings in this heaven can derive happiness from transformations. In the previous heaven of "happiness and contentment," the beings are happy and content regardless of whether there are transformations; they are content even in unhappy situations. In this heaven, the beings bring about happiness through transformations.

The sixth of the Desire Heavens is the Heaven of the Transformation of Others' Bliss (Paranirmita-vavartin). The beings of this heaven haven't any bliss of their own, but they can take it from beings in other heavens for their own enjoyment. Many demons live in this heaven along with their retinues. Why do they take the happiness of beings in other heavens? Because they are unreasonable. Common thieves in the world of men are generally gods fallen from the Heaven of the Transformation of Others' Bliss. Having fallen, they still have the habit of stealing money from others.

The Brahma Heavens include the Great Brahma (Mahabrahma) Heaven, the Multitudes of Brahma (Brahmakayika) Heaven, and the Ministers of Brahma (Brahmapurohita) Heaven. Beings of the Six Desire Heavens and the Brahma Heavens *practice the five precepts and the ten good deeds.*

Because these beings cultivated the five precepts and the ten good deeds, they obtain the blessings and rewards of the heavens. However, the cultivation of the five precepts and the ten good deeds plants good roots that have outflows, so the verse says: *Planting seeds with outflows.* It has nothing to do with anyone else at all. [Note: This last line is actually from the verse for the Dharma Realm of People.] You yourself are responsible.

It's not easy to explain the Dharma in the Sutras. When I speak, I don't prepare ahead of time. "The Master said it wrong," some of you are thinking, but you don't dare to say it aloud. However, once you say it in your mind, strangely enough, I receive your telegram. So I'll correct the last line: *They cannot terminate their transmigration.* Am I right this time? Did you say in your mind that I said it wrong? [Disciple: "Yes."] Ha! It wasn't just one person who thought that way. The rest of you should also admit it if you were having such thoughts. [Another disciple: "Yes, I was."] You have to be honest. If you aren't honest, you will never attain the Way. [Other disciples also admit that they were thinking that way.]

6) The Dharma Realm of Asuras

Asuras have a violent nature,
Laden with blessings, lacking power.
Absolutely determined to fight,
They bob along in karma's tow.

Asura is a Sanskrit word that means "ugly." Male *asuras* are extremely ugly; the females are beautiful. It is the nature of the male asura to initiate fights. The female *asura* is also naturally fond of fighting, but wages covert wars, unlike the overt physical battles of the males, using weapons of the mind such as jealousy, obstructiveness, ignorance, and affliction.

Sometimes this realm is included in the Three Good Realms—gods, humans, and *asuras.* At other times they are classified as one of the Four Evil Realms—hell-beings, hungry ghosts, animals, and *asuras.*

There are *asuras* in the animal realm, in the human realm, in the heavens, and among the hungry ghosts. Although the *asuras* are an individual Dharma Realm by themselves, they appear in the other realms as well. In general, regardless of what realm they are in, they like to pick fights, and they have bad tempers. They enjoy bossing others around and like to be supervisors, but they can't stand supervision. They won't be controlled by others. These are the characteristics of *asuras*.

If you haven't noticed the *asuras,* I can tell you more about them. Among people, *asuras* can be good or bad. The good *asuras* include military officials and troops, and bad *asuras* are bandits, thieves, robbers, thugs, murderers, and the like. We can see these *asuras* in the world of men.

There are also *asuras* in the heavens. Heavenly *asuras* wage battles against the heavenly troops of Shakra. From morning to night, they attempt to overthrow Shakra so that they can seize his jeweled throne and become the heavenly king. But no matter what strategy they use, they are always defeated, because they are "laden with blessings, lacking power." They have accumulated the blessings that earn them rebirth in the heavens, but they have no authority there. For that reason, they are invariably defeated in their battles with the heavenly troops.

Are there *asuras* in the animal realm? Yes. Tigers, for instance, are *asuras* among the animals. Lions and wolves are also *asuras* among the animals. These *asuras* bully the other animals. Wolves, tigers, and lions kill other animals for food. They prey on other animals because they have the nature of *asuras.* Snakes and eagles are also *asuras.*

In general, *asuras* are utterly unreasonable and have huge tempers. They are constantly blowing their tops. Too much temper!

There are also *asuras* in the hungry ghost realm, and they go around bullying other ghosts. The realm of hungry ghosts has kind ghosts and evil ghosts. Evil ghosts are utterly unreasonable. Ghosts are not reasonable to begin with, but these *asura* ghosts are even more unreasonable. And so the verse says: Asuras have a violent nature. They have explosive tempers.

Laden with blessings, lacking power. They have heavenly blessings, but lack heavenly authority. They fight for power and advantages, but fail to obtain them. *Absolutely determined to fight:* they love to fight and wage war. The modern world is a world of *asuras*—everyone is fighting and struggling, trying to knock each other down.

Asuras are so belligerent that they can keep fighting for one hundred, two hundred, three hundred, five hundred, or even a thousand years. They could fight for a thousand years without getting tired of it!

This is the Age Strong in Fighting and also the Dharma-Ending Age. Nevertheless, we don't want it to be the Dharma-Ending Age; we want the Proper Dharma to prevail. We should vow that wherever we go, the Proper Dharma will prevail. If we do that, every place we go will become a place of genuine Dharma. If everyone fulfilled this vow, the Dharma-Ending Age would become the Proper Dharma Age. We can turn the situation around.

They bob along in karma's tow. Asuras may be born in the heavens, in the human realm, or in the realms of animals and hungry ghosts. Dragged by the force of their karma, they become deluded, create more karma, and undergo the retribution. The force of their karma pulls them to undergo retribution in various realms. Cultivators should take care not to be belligerent and hot-tempered. Then they won't get dragged into the *asura* realm.

Five of the nine Dharma Realms have *asuras.* In the animal realm, there are *asuras* among creatures that fly in the air, those on the land, and those in the water. Crocodiles are an instance of *asuras* in the water. Wild stallions are *asuras* among horses. They bring trouble and disturbance to the herd. Most bulls are *asuras,* too. They butt their two horns against things to show their tough *asura* disposition. Bulls are *asuras* by nature. Dogs have even more of an *asura* nature, so people who own dogs are in close association with *asuras.* If you hang around *asuras,* you become closer to them. And getting close to them is dangerous; you might just fall into the realm of *asuras.* Everyone should pay attention to this and not run into the realm of *asuras!*

7) The Dharma Realm of People

> *The way of men is harmony,*
> *With merit and error interspersed.*
> *On virtuous deeds you rise; offenses make you fall.*
> *It has nothing to do with anyone else at all.*

The realm of *asuras* is dangerous, but what about the realm of people? There are both good and evil people. *The way of men is harmony.* People are harmonious beings who are capable of getting along with anyone.

However, those who become human beings are neither completely good nor completely bad. Beings who are completely good are reborn in the heavens, while those who are thoroughly bad become animals or hungry ghosts or fall into the hells. People have both merit and offenses. When a person's merit is greater than his offenses, he will be born into a rich and distinguished family, but one with small merit and heavy offenses will be born into a poor family. Between these extremes are a thousand differences and a myriad distinctions. Therefore, the verse says: *With merit and error interspersed.* They have some merit, and they also have some offenses; they are neither extremely yin nor extremely yang. Beings with a preponderance of yin become ghosts.

Those who are mostly yang become gods; they don't become humans.

Human beings can ascend to the heavens or fall into the hells. If you do good deeds, you ascend; if you commit offenses, you fall. So the verse says: *On virtuous deeds you rise; offenses make you fall.*

It has nothing to do with anyone else at all. Other people cannot tell you to fall into the hells, make you a ghost, or cause you to become an animal. It is entirely up to you. What you create you must endure. You must suffer the consequences of your own actions.

8) The Dharma Realm of Animals

Eager animals feed on greed,
Never sated by a lot.
They take what's black as white
And can't distinguish wrong from right.

The seven Dharma Realms discussed above are the better ones. If you wish, you can enter them to try them out—put on a play—but you shouldn't play around with the remaining three Dharma Realms. If you try these out, you may not be able to escape. It is said that once you lose your human form, ten thousand eons may pass before that form can be obtained again. It's very dangerous; you shouldn't treat it as mere play-acting. One of my disciples compared it to putting on a play, but he doesn't really understand what's going on.

There are billions of animals, an infinite variety—flying, crawling, swimming, or walking—in the sky, on land, and in the water. The species of birds and flying animals alone number in the millions, and land animals are not a few, either. There are millions of land animals ranging from small rodents through cows, horses, deer, and bears to the mighty elephant. In the water are seals, water buffalo, sea horses, manatees, and a myriad variety of swimming creatures.

We could never thoroughly study and understand all these animals. Even Ph.D.'s in the areas of zoology, biology, and related fields who do extensive and continuous research have no way to know all the animal species in the world. If they know a thousand, they don't know eleven hundred. If they know eleven hundred, they don't know twelve hundred.

Although someone might claim to know them all, how can he be certain that someone doesn't know more than he does? It's impossible to be sure. We have no way to completely know all the species of animals. Even the number of different kinds of insects would be hard to determine. When examined like that, wouldn't you say that the world is multilayered and infinite, infinite and multilayered?

Beings become animals as the result of one thing: greed. *Eager animals feed on greed.* For them, no matter what it is, the more the better. A little won't do. They are insatiably greedy; they never get tired of more.

Since they are *never sated by a lot,* they can't tell that black is black. They say, "Oh, it's white!" *They take what's black as white.* Because they are greedy for everything, they have no conceptions we consider reasonable—even to the point that they are greedy to eat excrement. The more excrement a dog eats, the better it likes it. People wonder how it can eat such filth, but the dog finds it more savory with every mouthful. That's how they are—never sated by a lot! That's an example of taking black as white: They delight in something that is basically unpleasant. Greed can extend even to the desire for more sickness. One sickness is not enough; they want two. They also want to take more medicine.

And they can't distinguish wrong from right. Animals are not clear about right and wrong, because they lack the ability to reason. How did they get that way? Simply through greed. They become muddled, and ignorance envelops them so that they become totally oblivious to anything rational.

Take heed, and don't be greedy. People who have left the home-life should not be greedy for money, but some say "the more the better!" Such greed puts you in grave danger, and it is easy to become an animal as a result.

"People who enter monastic life can't fall," you may say.

If they don't cultivate according to the Buddha's precepts, they will fall even faster. The ancients had a saying, "Many of those standing at the gates of the hells are Sanghans and Taoists." All the old Taoists and Buddhist monks who were greedy are waiting at the doors of hell saying, "Quick! Send me to the hells. Hurry up and let me come in!" Once in, it's a lot of fun inside. They think the hells will provide good entertainment, so they go there. But once they arrive they realize it is not a game.

9) The Dharma Realm of Hungry Ghosts

The ghostly crew delights in hate,
Deluded by effects, confused about cause;
Their ignorance and upside-downness
Grow greater each day, deeper each month.

Almost everyone has heard of ghosts, but not everyone believes in them. There are even Buddhist disciples who don't believe there are ghosts. Ghosts are masses of yin energy that have shadow and no form, or form and no shadow. Perhaps you have seen a dark shadow, but when you looked closer it disappeared. Or perhaps you've seen what seemed like a person, but which vanished in the blink of an eye. Such phenomena are difficult to understand.

Among the Ten Dharma Realms, we are now discussing the Dharma Realm of ghosts. There are as many different kinds of ghosts as there are grains of sand in the Ganges River. There are infinitely many kinds of ghosts. Some are affluent and powerful ghosts that reign as kings over the ghosts' realm. Some ghosts are poverty-stricken and devoid of authority—it is often the poor ghosts who bother people and go about causing trouble. If you want to know how many kinds of ghosts there are, work hard at cultivation, open the five eyes and six spiritual penetrations, and then you'll know.

As to people who say there are no ghosts, I tell them that if there are no ghosts, then there are also no Buddhas, people, or animals, because animals are transformed from ghosts, as are people, asuras, and so forth, even to gods, Arhats, Pratyekabuddhas, Bodhisattvas, and Buddhas. All realms come from the realm of ghosts, because the Ten Dharma Realms are not apart from a single thought of the mind, and one thought of the mind creates the Ten Dharma Realms.

By conducting yourself as if you were a ghost, you fall into the ghosts' realm. Acting as a person does, you come to the human realm. Behaving like an asura, you join the ranks of asuras. Assuming the practice of an Arhat, you enter the realm of Arhats. Behaving like One Enlightened to Conditions, you enter that realm. Doing the deeds of a Bodhisattva, you join the retinue of Bodhisattvas. Performing the work of a Buddha, you realize Buddhahood. If you commit hellish offenses, you fall into the hells. All of this is brought about by the one thought that is right now in your mind. Thus we say that the Ten Dharma Realms are not beyond a single thought.

The ghostly crew delights in hate. Ghosts enjoy exploding in a fiery rage when people are not good to them, and even when treated well they still get angry. They like nothing better than giving people trouble. They give you trouble whether you are good to them or not. There is an old saying: "Lighting a stick of incense calls forth ghosts." People light incense to pay respect to ghosts. Before you've paid respect to them they don't bother you, but once you make their acquaintance, the ghosts become a nuisance, make you sick, or give you some other trouble. Confucius said, "Respect the ghosts and spirits, but keep them at a distance." It is wise to pay respect to the ghosts and spirits, but otherwise keep your distance and don't get too close to them.

Deluded by effects, confused about cause. They are unclear about results and don't understand their causes. As a result, they can't tell good from bad. Basically if you plant a good cause, you reap a good fruit; if you plant a bad cause you reap a bad effect. If you plant melons you get melons; plant beans and you'll get beans. Ghosts don't understand that. They plant eggplant and anticipate eating hot peppers, or plant hot peppers and think they will harvest cucumbers. Since they have no comprehension of principles, they act recklessly and in confusion.

Their ignorance and upside-downness / Grow greater each day, deeper each month. They accumulate a lot karma every day. Their ignorance and upside-downness become deeper with each passing month. The more karma they create, the deeper their ignorance gets, and the deeper it gets, the more offenses they commit.

10) The Dharma Realm of Hell-beings

The hells' anxiety and suffering
Is devoid of doors, yet one bores right in.
Giving rise to delusion, deeds are done.
The retribution is borne in due accord.

The hells are a miserable place. Anyone who would like to take a vacation in the hells can do so any time at all. I can guarantee that you'll get there right away. How? It is said,

Depressed and melancholy, you roam through the hells.
Happy and smiling, you enjoy eternal youth.
Weeping and woe make a small dark room in the hells.

Once you become worried, you travel to the hells to take a vacation. If you get worried, you plant a seed for the hells. If you smile, you plant a seed for the heavens. It is said,

From ancient times, the divine immortals have had
no other practice
Than merely being happy and not being sad.

If you become depressed, you take a trip to the hells. If you smile all the time, you look youthful even if you are old. If you cry, you give yourself a lot of vexation.

In general, there is no happiness in the hells. They are full of suffering and distress. *The hells' anxiety and suffering / Is devoid of doors, yet one bores right in.* Unlike jails built to hold criminals, the hells haven't any doors. However, if you are due to go to hell, when you arrive it is just as if a door opened, because you find yourself worming and boring in where there was no entrance.

Giving rise to delusion, deeds are done. Why do you go to the hells? Ignorance and afflictions make you stupid and confused, so you create bad karma and don't do good deeds. *The retribution is borne in due accord.* When you create bad karma, you fall into the hells to undergo the retribution. There is no end to this cycle once it starts. You receive exact repayment for whatever karma you create, and the retribution is never off by even a hair's breadth.

All of these ten realms—a single thought—
Are not apart from your present thought.
If you can awaken to that thought,
You'll arrive immediately at the other shore.

Buddhas, Bodhisattvas, Hearers, and Those Enlightened to Conditions are the Four Sagely Dharma Realms; gods, human beings, asuras, hell-beings, hungry ghosts, and animals are the Six Common Dharma Realms. Together, they make up the Ten Dharma Realms. Where do the Ten Dharma Realms come from? From the single thought which is right now in your mind. All of these ten realms—a single thought—Are not apart from your present thought.

If you can awaken to that thought, if you can understand it, you'll arrive immediately at the other shore. The other shore is enlightenment. When you become enlightened, you are no longer confused. When ignorance is smashed and the Dharma-body appears, you arrive at the other shore. This is Mahaprajaparamita.

I've suddenly thought of the story of the "As-You-Wish Woman." She was a ghost that had been shattered by thunder in the Zhou Dynasty. She then practiced a kind of magic that protected her from thunder, and when she mastered it, she went around causing trouble. Later she met me, took refuge with the Triple Jewel, and reformed herself. I could write an entire book on this. You don't have to be afraid of her; even if she were to come here, she wouldn't harm anyone.

Twenty-seven years ago [1945], on the twelfth day of the second month, I passed through the Zhou family station in Manchuria. In the town there was a Virtue Society whose members met daily for lectures on morality. Since some of the members were my disciples, I would usually stay in the town for a few days when I passed through.

This time I met a Chinese astrologer who cast people's horoscopes by looking at the eight characters (two for the year, two for the month, two for the day, and two for the hour) of their birth. His horoscopes were very efficacious. He cast my horoscope and said, "You should be an official. Why have you left home? Had you wanted to, you could have been a great official."

"I haven't any idea how to be an official," I said. "But I do know how to be a Buddhist monk, and so I have left home."

"What a pity," said the astrologer, and he looked at my hands. "At the very least," he said, "you could have been a top-ranking imperial scholar."

"No," I said. "I couldn't even have come in last."

He looked my hands again and said, "Oh, this year something very lucky will happen to change your life!"

"What could that be?" I asked.

"After the tenth of the next month you will be different from now," he replied.

"Different in what way?"

"Right now, all the people within 1,000 li [350 miles] believe in you, but after the tenth of next month, everyone within 10,000 li [3,500 miles] will believe in you."

"How can that be?" I asked.

"When the time comes, you will know," he said.

Two days later, on the fourteenth or fifteenth of the second month, I went to the village of Xiangbaichi, fourth district, and stayed with my disciple Xia Zunxiang, who was over sixty years old and had a family of over thirty people. He was one of the richest landowners in the area and had never believed in Buddhism or anything else. But when he saw me, he believed in me and wanted to take refuge with me. He and his whole family took refuge, and every time I went to the village I'd stay at his house. His family of over thirty was extremely happy to see me this time. I stayed with them for ten days, and about seventy-two people came to take refuge.

On the twenty-fifth, I set out in Mr. Xia's cart for Shuangcheng County. Since it was over seventy li [25 miles] away, we left at three o'clock in the morning.

Although it was early spring, the weather was bitter cold. The driver and the attendant were dressed in fur coats, trousers, and hats. Being very poor, I wore only my usual rag robe made of three layers of thin cotton cloth, trousers made of two layers of cloth, open Arhat sandals with no socks, and a hat shaped like folded palms that didn't cover my ears. That was the kind of hat that Master Ji Gong wore.

We rode from three in the morning until dawn, reaching the city at seven in the morning. The driver and the attendant thought I would freeze to death since I was so insufficiently dressed. They had stopped repeatedly to exercise and keep warm, but I had remained in the cart from the beginning of the trip. When we arrived at the eastern gate of Shuangcheng County and I got out of the cart, the driver exclaimed, "Oh, we thought surely you had frozen to death!"

I stayed with friends, Dharma protecting laymen, for more than ten days, and on the ninth of the third month, I returned to Xia Zunxiang's home in Xiangbaichi. When I arrived, he told me that one of my recent disciples, the daughter of Xia Wenshan, had fallen dangerously ill. She hadn't eaten or drunk water for six or seven days. She did not speak, and she looked fiercely angry, as if she wanted to beat people.

Then her mother came. "Master," she said, "my daughter became very ill a few days after taking refuge. She won't talk, eat, or drink, but just glares and sticks her head on the bed. I don't know what illness she has."

I said to her, "I can't cure her, so it's useless to ask me. However, my disciple Han Gangji has opened his five eyes and knows people's past, present, and future affairs. You should ask him."

Han Gangji had also taken refuge on the twenty-fourth of the second month. At first I had refused to take him as a disciple, because before I had left home, the two of us had been good friends and had worked together in the Virtue Society. After I left home and Han Gangji opened his five eyes, he saw that, life after life, I had always been his teacher. And so he wanted to take refuge with me.

I said, "We're good friends; how could I take you as a disciple?"

"But if I don't take refuge with you, I shall certainly fall in this life," Han Gangji said, and he knelt on the ground and refused to get up.

I was just as determined not to accept him, but after perhaps half an hour, I finally said, "Those who take refuge with me must follow instructions. You have talent; you know the past, present, and future. Is it possible that it has caused you to become arrogant? Will your pride prevent you from obeying my instructions?"

"Master," he said, "I'll certainly obey. If you tell me to throw myself into a cauldron of boiling water, I'll do it. If you tell me to walk on fire, I'll walk. If I get boiled or burned to death, that's all right."

"You'd better be telling the truth," I said. "If I give you instructions, you can't ignore them."

"No matter what it is," he said, "if you tell me to do it, I will do it, and fear no danger whatsoever."

And so Han Gangji was one of the seventy-two people who took refuge on the twenty-fourth.

Hearing that one of my disciples was sick, I told Han Gangji, "You can diagnose illnesses. Take a look."

Han Gangji sat in meditation and made a contemplative examination of the illness. Suddenly his face blanched with terror. "Master," he said, "we can't handle this one. It's beyond our control."

"What is it?" I asked.

"The demon who is causing the illness is extremely violent and can assume human form to bring chaos into the world and injury to humankind."

"What makes the demon so fierce?" I asked.

"The demon was a ghost long ago in the Zhou Dynasty," he said. "Because it didn't behave properly, a virtuous man with spiritual powers shattered it with thunder. But the ghost's spirit did not completely disperse, and it later fused into a powerful demon that could fly and vanish and appear again, at will."

"The demon has refined a magic weapon," he continued. "It's an exclusive anti-thunder device: a black hat made out of the thin membranes that cover the bodies of newborn children. When she wears the hat, the thunder cannot hurt her, because thunder has a great aversion to filth."

Westerners think that thunder has no one controlling it, and while that may be the case for ordinary thunder, there is a special kind of thunder that is used by gods to punish the goblins, demons, and ghosts who wander throughout the world.

In addition to the black hat, which protected her from thunder, she had refined two other magic weapons: two round balls. If she put her hat on someone, his soul would fall under her control, and he would become one of her followers. If she hit someone with one of the two round balls, he would immediately die.

Han Gangji saw that she was such a fierce demon and said, "Master, we can't handle this one."

"Then what will become of the sick girl?" I asked.

"She will certainly die; there's no way to help her," he said.

"I can't allow her to die. If she weren't my disciple I'd pay no attention, but she took refuge with me on the twenty-fourth of last month."

When those people had taken refuge, I had taught them to recite the Great Compassion Mantra. I had said to them, "Each of you should learn to recite the Great Compassion Mantra. It will be of great help to you. If you are in danger and distress and you recite it, Guanyin Bodhisattva will protect you." Since then, many of them had been reciting the Great Compassion Mantra.

I said, "If she hadn't taken refuge with me, I wouldn't care whether the demon took her life or not. But she took refuge with me, so I can't allow the demon to take her life. I've got to do something."

"You take care of it, then," said Han Gangji, "but I'm not going."

"What?" I said, "When you took refuge, you promised me that you would jump into boiling water or walk on fire if I asked you to. Now it's not even boiling water or fire; why have you decided to back out?"

Han Gangji had nothing to say. He thought it over. "If you appoint some Dharma-protecting gods to take care of me…"

"Don't shilly-shally!" I said. "If you're going to go, go. But don't vacillate!"

He said no more and followed me. When we arrived, the girl was lying on the bed with her head on the pillow and her bottom sticking up in the air; it was an embarrassing sight. Her eyes were as wide as those of a cow, and she glared with rage at me.

I asked the girl's family, "What is the cause of the illness?"

They told me that seven or eight days earlier, an old woman, around age fifty, had been sitting beside an isolated grave outside the village. She was wearing a dark blue gown and had braided her hair backwards in two plaits that went up her head in back and hung down across her temples. She was wearing yellow trousers and shoes, and she was crying mournfully beside the grave. Hearing her cries, the elderly Mrs. Xia went to comfort her, but she continued to cry, "Oh my person, oh my person…" and kept looking for her "person."

Finally she stopped crying, and the two of them walked to the village gate. There must have been a spirit guarding the gate, because the old woman wouldn't go in. The village was surrounded by a wall and had a gate on each of the four sides. Mrs. Xia went in, but the old woman stayed outside the gate, crying.

At that moment Xia Zunxiang's horse cart returned to the village. When it reached the gate the horse saw the woman and shied in fright, for horses can recognize things that people cannot see. As the horse cart went careening through the gate, the old woman followed it in. Probably the spirit who guarded the gate had his back turned, and in the confusion, she went sneaking through.

The old woman ran to the house of Mr. Yu Zhongbao and continued to look for her "person." She looked at Mr. Yu and then ran out of the house, where she was surrounded by thirty or forty curious onlookers who jeered at her, "Stupid old woman! What's your last name?"

"I don't have a last name."

"What's your first name?" they asked.

"I don't know. I'm a corpse," she said. They looked at her as if she were a freak. She continued to walk as if in a stupor until she reached the back wall of Xia Wenshan's estate. She then threw her hat over the eight-foot wall, and in one jump, leapt right over after it. No one else could have jumped over the wall, but she made it.

"The stupid old woman knows kung fu!" the crowd screeched, and they ran around and went in through the front gate to watch her.

Xia Wenshan's son Xia Zunquan, who had also taken refuge on the twenty-fourth, ran in the door. "Mama! Mama! The stupid old woman is in our house, but don't be afraid."

His mother looked out the window, but saw nothing strange. When she turned around, there was the old woman crawling up on the brick bed. She was halfway on the bed and halfway on the floor.

"What do you want?" shouted the mother, but the old woman made no reply.

Seeing the old woman's strange behavior, the mother and her daughter began immediately to recite the mantra. Just as they recited the first line of the mantra, *Na mo he la da nuo duo la ye ye,* the old woman slipped to the ground and lay inert, exactly like a corpse.

Seeing that, the family was greatly upset. If somebody were to die in their home, it would not be good.

They went for the sheriff. When the sheriff saw the old woman lying on the floor as if she were dying, he picked her up with one hand and set her outside. Then he took her to the village courthouse for questioning. "Where are you from?" he asked, "and why have you come here?"

"Don't ask me," she said. "I'm a corpse. I have no name and no home. I just live wherever I am."

Frightened by her strange talk and behavior, the sheriff escorted her at pistol point some fifty paces outside the village. But when he returned to the village gate, she was right behind him. He took her seventy paces, and she followed him back again. Finally, he and three deputies took her 150 paces outside the village and said, "Get out or get shot!" and they fired two shots in the air.

The old woman fell to the ground in terror, thinking the shots were thunder, which had destroyed her before. This time she didn't follow them back to the village.

When the sheriff and his men returned, they heard that Xia Wenshan's daughter was sick—not speaking, eating, or sleeping, but just lying on the bed staring in rage with her head on the pillow and her bottom sticking up in the air. She didn't eat for seven or eight days.

Before we went to Xia Wenshan's home, I said to Han Gangji, "You said that if we tried to handle the matter we would die. Well, I would rather die than not save one of my disciples. First of all, I must save those who have taken refuge with me; I can't just stand by and let them die. Secondly, I must save the demon. You say no one can control her, but she has committed so many offenses there's bound to be someone who can subdue her. If she were to be destroyed, it would be a great pity, for she has cultivated diligently for many years. Even if she has enough power to kill me, I'll still save her. Finally, I must save all living beings in the world, and if I don't subdue her now, in the future many people will be harmed by her. For these three reasons, then, I'm going to work."

Just then the sheriff happened to pass by and overheard us saying that the old woman was a demon. "No wonder!" he exclaimed. "That's why I was able to pick her up with one hand, just as if there were nothing there at all. It didn't occur to me at the time, but now I realize she's a demon."

We then had to find the demon. How did we do that? There are five kinds of dharmas in the Shurangama Mantra. One is the dharma for extinguishing calamities. If you are due to suffer a calamity, you can use this dharma to avert it. There is also the dharma for creating auspiciousness, which turns inauspicious events into auspicious ones. With the dharma of summoning and hooking, you can catch goblins, demons, and ghosts no matter how far away they are. There is also the dharma of subduing and conquering, which allows you to subdue any demon that comes. I employed these dharmas from the Shurangama Mantra to summon the As-You-Wish demon woman.

When she entered the room, she had about her an intense and nauseating stench. She came in and tried to put her magic weapon—the black hat—on my head, but couldn't get it on me. Then she took out her round balls and tried to hit me, but they missed my body.

Both of her magic weapons had failed. Knowing she was finished, she turned to run, but when she first arrived, I had set up an invisible boundary that would trap her no matter where she tried to go. The gods, dragons, and others of the eightfold division of Dharma-protectors watched her from the left, right, front, rear, above, and below. Seeing that she couldn't get away, she knelt and wept.

I then spoke the Dharma for her. I explained the Four Noble Truths, the Twelve Causes and Conditions, and the Six Perfections. She immediately understood, resolved to realize Bodhi, and asked to take refuge with the Triple Jewel. I accepted her and gave her the name Vajra As-You-Will Maiden.

She followed me around to save people, but her basic make-up was that of a demon, and no matter where she went she carried her overwhelming stench. Seeing that it wouldn't do for her to follow me, I sent her to Leifa Mountain in Jiaohe County, Jilin Province, to cultivate in the Exquisite Cave of the Ten Thousand Saints.

EXQUISITE CAVE OF TEN THOUSAND SAINTS

Why is the cave called the "Exquisite Cave of the Ten Thousand Saints"?

I HAVE sent many of my strange and unusual disciples there to cultivate, and I have also been there myself. She cultivated vigorously and soon attained spiritual powers and could rescue people. When she rescued them, she didn't like it to be known, since good done hoping others will know is not true good, and evil done in secret for fear that others will know is truly great evil.

Thus, the former demon woman became one of the Buddha's followers.

Why is the cave called the "Exquisite Cave of the Ten Thousand Saints"? It's said to be exquisite because it has three entrances, which are mutually visible to each other. It's like a glass cup, in that one can see in from the outside and out from the inside. The three entrances to the cave are mutually connected. Inside the cave there is a temple made of bricks and lumber that were carried up the steep mountain crags on the backs of goats. One goat could carry two bricks or a piece of lumber at a time. Off the western entrance of the cave, there is another cave called the Cave of Lao Zi. Off the eastern entrance is the Dripping Water Cave, which drips enough water to satisfy a troop of ten thousand men and horses. The cave in the back is called the Cave of Patriarch Ji, named after Ji Xiaotang, a native of Manchuria who, in the Ming Dynasty, subdued five ghosts, one of whom was the Black Fish Spirit. The Black Fish Spirit was a Ming Dynasty official in Beijing called Blackie the Great. His last name was Black, but he wasn't a human; he was a fish. Ji Xiaotang knew this and was determined to capture him. He knew that "Blackie" would pass by the mountain one day, and so he waited for him. When he passed by, Ji Xiaotang released thunder from the palm of his hand and killed him.

No one actually knows how many caves there are in Leifa Mountain. Each time you count them, the number is different—seventy-two today, seventy-three tomorrow, and maybe seventy the day after that.

A man once went there and saw two old men playing chess in a cave. When he coughed, the two long-bearded men said to themselves,

"How did he get here?" and then the stone gate of the entrance closed by itself. The man knelt there seeking the truth from them until he finally died. His grave may still be seen outside the Stone Door Cave. How sincerely he sought for the truth!

There are many spirits and immortals up in the mountain. One was a man named Lee Mingfu, who had mastered martial arts and could run as fast as a monkey. Once I visited the cave at four in the morning and saw him bowing to the Buddha. His hair, which he never washed, was held by a hairpin and matted in a lump that weighed five or six pounds. His facial features—eyes, nose, and mouth—and his body, were very small, but his body was strong. He alone could carry two railroad tracks so heavy that eight ordinary men would be needed to carry one; he would tuck one track under each arm. No one knew how old he was or where he was from. He was one of the strange men I met there.

These are not stories that I made up; they are true events. If you believe them, fine. If you don't believe, that's also fine. It's all up to you.

STEADFAST PERSEVERENCE

Cultivation is not a one-day affair. Rather, we must cultivate in thought after thought, from morning to night, year and month after month.

A TREE grows bigger day by day, even though we may not notice it. After a few decades or a century, a tree can make good lumber. Cultivation of the Way is like the growing tree, it happens gradually. Don't be in a rush, thinking that you can cultivate today and become enlightened tomorrow. It's not that easy. You must train and cultivate every day. Don't worry about how much progress you're making. As long as you don't retreat, you're making progress. If you have fewer random thoughts each day, then you're making progress.

> *One who makes rapid progress will also beat a hasty retreat.*

Those who advance quickly will also be quick to retreat. Cultivate with constant and steadfast resolve. Each day, we should strive to repent, correct our errors, and turn over a new leaf. As it's said,

> *A day of having corrected no faults*
> *Is a day of having created no merit.*

We are cultivating to get rid of bad habits and faults, to cease having defiled thoughts, and reveal our inherent clarity and wisdom. The wisdom and clarity are there, but they have been covered up by ignorance, so we cannot make good use of them. When we are obscured by ignorance, we tend to become petty and mean. If our wisdom comes forth, we will become more noble and go against the common flow. Cultivation is not a one-day affair. Rather, we must cultivate in thought after thought, from morning to night, year after year and month after month, with unchanging perseverance. Eventually, our Prajna wisdom will mature. Don't "sun it for one day and freeze it for ten" — you'll never accomplish anything that way. We should cultivate sincerely every day, just as a tree grows slowly but surely.

As we practice, we should remain calm whether we encounter demonic obstacles, adverse situations, or even favorable situations. Both in adversity and smooth situations, we should maintain our vigor. If we can recognize all things as proclaiming the wonderful Dharma, we will see ineffable wonders. By cultivating the transcendental Dharma right within worldly affairs, we can take the road home and discover our true identity.

At that point nothing will confuse us. When states arise, we will be able solve the problems easily. No situation will obstruct us. Eventually, our wisdom will come forth. It hasn't come forth yet because we aren't able to see through things and let go of them. Thus we cannot be free and at ease. We have been backsliding instead of advancing. When we encounter good conditions, we hesitate and feel unsure of ourselves. Meeting evil conditions, we follow right along and drift aimlessly in the six paths, sinking deeper and deeper, unable to escape. We linger on, thinking it's a lot of fun, so we go through birth, death, and rebirth. We are born muddled, die confused, and don't know what we're doing in between. We can't figure out what life is all about.

We lived muddled lives, thinking we have achieved fame, fortune, and success. Sages see our worldly success as failure. We should carefully look into what we have done, examine our accounts, and truly understand the situation. Once we understand, we can be true heroes and leap out from the endless cycle of birth and death.

A talk given on June 6, 1982
at the City of Ten Thousand Buddhas

DON'T WAIT TO CULTIVATE

In his quest for perfect wisdom, the Buddha dedicated his life to vigorous cultivation. How can we expect to achieve Buddhahood without any effort at all"

SHAKYAMUNI BUDDHA "cultivated blessings and wisdom for three *asamkhyeyas* of eons, and planted the causes for his hallmarks and characteristics for a hundred eons." He undertook ascetic practices, doing what was difficult to do and enduring what was difficult to endure. He sought enlightenment and universal wisdom, and committed his life to teaching beings. In life after life, he toiled and suffered, eating what others could not eat, yielding where others could not yield. Eventually he accomplished Buddhahood.

The Buddha didn't attain Buddhahood overnight. He cultivated for three great *asamkhyeyas* of eons before manifesting the Eight Signs of Attaining the Way. The first sign is the descent from the Tushita Heaven. The Tushita Heaven is where the Dharma Prince who will become the next Buddha dwells. The second sign is that of entering the womb. The third is that of dwelling in the womb. Even while in the womb, the Buddha turned the Dharma wheel and taught those beings with whom he had affinities. The fourth sign is that of birth. The Buddha was born on the eighth day of the fourth lunar month. After he came out of the womb, he pointed one hand toward the heavens and one hand toward the earth, and said, "In the heavens above and the earth below, I alone am honored."

Was the Buddha being arrogant? I'm not acting like the Buddha's defense attorney, but the answer is no, since the Buddha was indeed qualified to say that. He said it to let beings know who he was.

On the day that the Buddha was born, nine dragons spouted water to bathe him. Being born as a prince, he began learning worldly skills in the palace. The prince mastered the skills of ordinary people without having to learn them. Later upon walking out of the four gates of the palace, the young prince witnessed birth, old age, sickness, and death and felt that these were great sufferings. He saw that everything comes into being, lasts for a while, and then decays and becomes extinct. Regarding the sufferings of birth, old age, sickness, and death as bleak and meaningless, he resolutely renounced his royal position and left the home-life.

We can say that the Buddha was the foremost practitioner of ascetism. For six years in the Himalayas, he cultivated vigorously while living on a daily fare of one sesame seed and one grain of wheat. He certainly didn't take vitamin supplements.

Later, he accepted an offering of porridge with milk offered by a shepherdess. When he went to sit in meditation beneath the Bodhi tree, he made a vow: "I will not rise from here until I have attained Proper, Equal and Right Enlightenment." He sat there for forty-nine days, and then saw a star at midnight and awakened to the Way. He suddenly realized the original, pure, wonderfully bright, true mind which knows neither birth nor death, neither defilement nor purity, neither increase nor decrease.

This is the age of the Dharma's decline, and we must be true disciples of the Buddha. In the past, our forefather, the Buddha, did not take it easy in his cultivation. Even though we cannot live on one sesame seed and one grain of wheat a day, we should not crave good food either. We should not be greedy for vitamin supplements or rich food.

This body is a stinking skin bag; it is only a false combination of the four elements. We have been slaves to our bodies long enough; we have committed too many offenses on its behalf. If we still can't see through the body and put it down, and we continue to slave and toil for it, we're really wasting our time. Therefore, we should understand that life is full of suffering, and then we should study Buddhism in order to return to the source. Only by realizing sagehood and becoming a Buddha can we find true happiness.

In remembering the Buddha's birthday, and we should learn to be like the Buddha. We should take the Buddha's body as our own body, the Buddha's conduct as our own conduct, the Buddha's mind as our own mind, the Buddha's vows as our own vows, and the Buddha's will as our own will. We should bear the toil and hardship, and emulate the Buddha's indomitable spirit. Anyone who can be this way has a chance to become a Buddha, and will quickly be able to end birth and death.

In his quest for perfect wisdom, the Buddha dedicated his life to vigorous cultivation. How can we expect to achieve Buddhahood without exerting any effort at all? If we monastics don't cultivate seriously, how can we face the Buddhas, Bodhisattvas, and our ancestors? If we are greedy and contentious, pursue fame and profit, and become more and more selfish, how can we face our parents and ancestors? We should be considerate towards others, and not just care about ourselves. We must muster our spirits and cultivate. We can't put it off until tomorrow, for who knows when the ghost of impermanence will arrive? When he comes, we may want to live for a few more days, but it won't be possible.

Don't wait until you're old to cultivate the Way.
The lonely graves are filled with young people.

In this world, we are born and we die, and after dying we are born again. If we don't live virtuously, we may be reborn as animals. Once we lose the human body, we may not recover it for ten thousand eons. Don't fool yourself into thinking you don't need to cultivate because the Buddha can help you attain Buddhahood. Take a lesson from Ananda: He was the Buddha's cousin, but the Buddha couldn't give him samadhi. He still had to diligently apply himself to his own cultivation.

A talk given on May 1, 1982
at the City of Ten Thousand Buddhas

LIFE IS BUT A DREAM

Now we will discuss some of the richest, the noblest, the poorest, and the lowliest figures in Chinese history.

Shi Chong was wealthy,
and Fan Dan, poor;
Gan Luo's fate was to be late,
while Tai Gong was early.
Peng Zu was long-lived,
but Yan's life was short.
These six people are all within
the five elements.

SHI CHONG, who lived in the Jin Dynasty, was one of the wealthiest and most famous people in Chinese history. His fortune was comparable to the national treasury. Once Shi Chong went to a banquet at a friend's house. His friend told him how he had obtained a coral "tree" two feet eight inches high and then brought the piece out to show Shi Chong.

Shi Chong took a look and scoffed, "What's so great about that?" He then stomped on the coral tree and smashed it to bits.

"Oh no!" his friend cried ruefully. "It was so hard to find in the first place, and now you've ruined it. How awful!"

Shi Chong retorted, "What's the big deal? I've got zillions like this in the storerooms at home. Come see for yourself."

The friend went to Shi Chong's house where he saw several hundred coral clusters over three feet tall.

Shi Chong said, "Go ahead! Take one! Choose whichever one you like!" What his friend had prized as a treasure was a dime a dozen in Shi Chong's house. This shows how tremendously wealthy Shi Chong was. No one knew the true extent of his fortune.

Fan Dan was a beggar who had nothing of his own. Each day he would go out and beg for his food, and then he would eat however much he got. He didn't work at all. When he ran out of food, he would go and beg for more. His situation was such that:

Barely getting by on a day's scraps,
He was on the verge of homelessness.

Every place was home to him. Although it was true that Fan Dan was poor and always had to beg for food, he probably started saving up some food. Confucius and his disciples ran out of food when they were travelling through the state of Chen. Since they had nothing to eat, Confucius told his disciple Zi Lu to go and borrow some rice from Fan Dan.

Confucius had so many followers, and yet he needed to borrow rice from a beggar, strange how things work, isn't it? Zi Lu went to Fan Dan and explained, "My teacher has run out of food in the state of Chen, and I've come to borrow rice from you."

Fan Dan said, "If you want to borrow rice, that's fine, but first you must answer my question. If you give the right answer, I'll lend you the rice. If you don't, I won't lend it to you."

Zi Lu confidently replied, "Ask away!"

Fan Dan said, "Tell me, in this world, what is numerous and what is few? What makes people happy and what makes them sad? If you tell me the right answer, I'll lend you the rice with no strings attached. You can borrow as much as you want. If you answer wrongly, however, I won't lend the rice to you. I have to make that clear first."

Zi Lu said, "Your question is way too easy! In this world, there are many stars and few moons. Weddings are happy and deaths are sad."

When Fan Dan heard Zi Lu's answer, he waved his hand and said, "Wrong!"

Zi Lu felt that his answer was perfect, that none could be better. He was sure that Fan Dan hadn't planned to lend him the rice to begin with and had just been teasing. So, he refused to admit defeat. But Fan Dan still wouldn't lend him the rice. Since there was nothing he could do about it, he left in exasperation and went to see Confucius.

"Teacher! Teacher! That Fan Dan is truly abominable! He wasn't reasonable at all." Zi Lu faithfully reported the entire conversation to Confucius. Confucius said, "You did give the wrong answer!"

Zi Lu was completely taken aback and protested, "Fan Dan said I was wrong, because he was arguing for himself. But Teacher, you should be on my side! Why do you say that I'm wrong as well?"

Confucius said, "Listen to my answer: 'In this world, there are many petty people and few noble people. People are happy when they borrow things but sad when asked to return them.' Go give Fan Dan that answer." Zi Lu went back to Fan Dan and repeated Confucius' answer to him. Fan Dan considered this answer to be completely correct, so he lent the rice to Zi Lu. He filled a bamboo tube with rice and gave it to Zi Lu to take back. This bamboo tube was actually a magic treasure that provided an endless supply of rice. No matter how much rice one wanted to use, the tube could provide that amount. You see, poor men also have their poor men's treasures.

During the reign of the First Emperor of the Qin Dynasty, a boy named Gan Luo was made prime minister when he was only twelve. He should have become prime minister at the age of nine, but he was late by three years. Jiang Tai Gong [a sage who lived during the time of King Wen of the Zhou Dynasty] didn't meet King Wen until he was eighty. Even so, he was early by three years. Gan Luo became the prime minister at a very young age, but Jiang Tai Gong didn't meet King Wen until late in life.

Peng Zu lived for over eight hundred years, so he is considered to have been long-lived. Confucius' disciple, Yan Yuan, on the other hand, died at age thirty, so he's said to have been short-lived. Even so, he was the most intelligent of Confucius' disciples, and the most avid learner. Upon learning one principle, he could deduce ten others. When Zi Gong (another disciple) heard one principle, he could only deduce two. At Yan Yuan's death, Confucius lamented, "Heaven is destroying me! Heaven is destroying me!" What he meant was, "Heaven has doomed my teaching! Heaven has doomed my teaching!"

These six people include some of the richest, poorest, most noble, and most long-lived people, and also one whose life was rather short. However, none of them was able to transcend his fate, which was determined by the five elements. None of them could escape the endless cycle of transmigration. Life is just like a dream, an illusion, a bubble, a shadow, a dewdrop, or a lightning flash; that's how we ought to contemplate. Be attached to nothing and you will have no affliction. If you can see through everything, put it all down, and come here to cultivate, that's even better. If you can't put everything down right away, then let go of things little by little. Don't hanker after this transient existence in the six paths.

A talk given on June 6, 1982
at the City of Ten Thousand Buddhas

ALL THINGS ARE IMPERMANENT

The Buddha doesn't crave the things that worldly people crave. The Buddha doesn't love the things that worldly people love. Since he is free of greed and love, he has no affliction.

ALTHOUGH the Buddha was a prince in India, he was deeply weary of worldly fortune and honor. He wanted to renounce the glory of his royal position and leave the home-life to cultivate the Way. He wished to make all living beings realize that worldly dharmas are nothing but false thoughts. How did the world come into being? It was created by the false thoughts of living beings, and in the future it will be destroyed by the false thoughts of living beings. This is the correspondence between cause and effect.

All things in the world are impermanent and subject to decay. Bodhisattvas detest worldly dharmas, and Buddhas detest worldly dharmas even more. They are not defiled by craving for them, and they are not attached to them. The Buddha has forever ended the greed, love, and desires that worldly people feel. The Buddha doesn't crave the things that worldly people crave. The Buddha doesn't love the things that worldly people love. Since he is free of greed and love, he has no affliction. Our afflictions come from our greed and love. Without greed, we won't be selfish; and without selfishness, we won't be afflicted. When we feel greed and love, and things do not go as we wish, we become afflicted. Once we are afflicted, we become muddled. Once we are muddled, we are defiled. When we cultivate pure conduct, we destroy all defilements.

The Buddha was able to constantly benefit all living beings. When the Buddha was still living in the palace, he did not covet sensual pleasures, nor did he crave worldly splendor, wealth, and honor. After he left the home-life, he completely renounced the behavior of worldly people. He refrained from contending and arguing with people, and thus attained the samadhi of non-contention. As it is said,

Contention involves thoughts of winning and losing;
It goes against the Way.
Thinking about the four marks,
How can one attain samadhi?

The Buddha fulfilled the vows he had made in the past and became endowed with limitless merit and virtue. With the light of great wisdom, he eradicated all the stupidity and darkness in the world. He served as a supreme field of blessings for living beings in the world. On behalf of all living beings, he constantly praised the merit and virtue of all Buddhas throughout the ten directions and three periods of time.

Thus he enabled all living beings to cultivate blessings, seek wisdom, and plant various roots of goodness by drawing near to the Triple Jewel. The Buddha used his Wisdom Eye to contemplate genuine truth. On behalf of all living beings, he also praised the merit and virtue of leaving the home-life.

Leaving home means leaving the home of the Three Realms: the Desire Realm, the Form Realm, and the Formless Realm. It also means leaving the home of an ordinary person in the world. One leaves behind one's worldly ideas. It also means leaving the home of affliction. Every person in the world dwells in the home of affliction. When we lose our tempers, we feel it tastes more flavorful than any delicious food we could eat. Therefore, when we leave home, we mean to leave the home of affliction. We should also leave the home of ignorance. Because of ignorance, we don't understand anything, and all of our actions and deeds are deluded. So we ought to leave the home of ignorance.

People leave the home-life for various reasons. For example, in China, some people leave the home-life because they are old and have no one to support them, and leaving home makes it easier to get meals. Others are forced by circumstances to leave the home-life. Perhaps someone has broken the law or committed murder, so he changes his name and leaves the home-life. Then the authorities pay no more attention to him, and they cannot track him down, either. Some children are sent to a temple to leave the home-life because their families have difficulty raising them.

It is not certain whether people who leave the home-life for the above three reasons will be able to cultivate. They may or they may not be able to. Finally, there is the person who leaves the home-life because he genuinely wants to end birth and death. If such a left-home person doesn't retreat from his resolve, he will be able to cultivate. Being painfully aware of birth and death, he will make the great resolve to reach enlightenment and cultivate according to the Dharma spoken by the Buddha. There are various situations under which people leave the home-life. After leaving the home-life, you should purify yourself of offenses and get rid of all your faults. Stay away from offenses and put an end to evil deeds. Regain your original purity. Leave the home of the Triple Realm, the home of affliction, the home of ignorance, and the worldly home forever.

Question: Why are there no female Buddhas?

Answer: That's not quite true. As the *Dharma Flower Sutra* says, the Dragon Girl offered her precious pearl to the Buddha and immediately attained Buddhahood. This proves that those in female bodies can also become Buddhas; however, it is quite rare. As to why some are born to become men and others women, it's a question of personal preference. If one longs to be a woman, one will become a woman. If one likes to be a man, one will become a man. Your karma controls you, and you undergo the retribution of the karma you create.

Nevertheless, some people can control their own karma. Instead of being turned around by a situation, they can turn the situation around. They can alter their karma and be their own masters. If you follow your karma, you are not in control. But if you can direct your karma, then you are in control. Why do Bodhisattvas make vows? Because they want to control the flow of their karma. Relying on their great vows as a foundation, they can direct their karma. In their case, they can control their karma, but their karma cannot control them. They can control states of mind, but states of mind cannot control them. They can control their retribution, but retribution cannot control them. One can control these things, but only with wisdom. Someone who is always stupid and ignorant and doing muddled things will not be able to control his karma. When asked why you do muddled things, you answer that you don't know. Your not knowing means you are being led by your karma.

It is not the case that women cannot become Buddhas. You could say that Buddhas are purely yang and ghosts are purely yin. People are partly yin and partly yang. It is not the case that men are completely yang and women are completely yin. If men were completely yang, they would not need to marry women, and if women were completely yin, they would not need to marry men. After marriage, people become partly yin and partly yang and are no longer purely one or the other. When you reach a state of being without outflows, you are purely yang. Although men are yang, there is yin within the yang. Although women are yin, there is yang within the yin. Therefore, when a man and woman are married, they are able to have children: these are all transformations of yin and yang. It is not a fixed rule that men are definitely yang and women are definitely yin. The *Book of Changes* says,

> *A balance of yin and yang is the Way.*
> *An excess of either yin or yang is sickness.*

An excess on either side will cause problems. What is not excessive in either direction is called the "middle." What admits of no change is "constant." This is the Way of the "constant middle." Therefore, men should not think they are yang. If you were, why would you want to get married? After you are married, there is yin within the yang. After women are married, there is yang within the yin. There is a mutual interchange. That's yin and yang.

As to what a person is, a "person" is merely a false name. We use the word "person," but, when language was invented, if the word "dog" had been applied to people, people would be called dogs now. Names of things become habitual. So "person" is a mere name. It is said that one yin and one yang make a person. Within the yang there is yin, and within the yin there is yang. Summer is included in winter, and winter is hidden in summer. On the day of the winter solstice, yang is born. On the day of the summer solstice, yin is born. A year is divided into yin and yang. When the yin reaches an extreme, it becomes yang. When the yang reaches the utmost point, it becomes yin. When people are born, they are yang, and when they die, they become yin. It's the same principle.

You say we are called "people," but if in the beginning people had been called chickens, then we would be called by the name of "chicken." After we became used to being called that, we wouldn't feel it was so strange. For example, if you give a child the name "Little Dog," then when he grows up and someone calls out, "Little Dog," he will know he is being called. That's just a false name, nothing more. If you ask a man named Smith why his name is Smith, he will say it's because his father's name is Smith. What was his father's father's name? It was also Smith. How about his father's father's father? Keep tracing the generations back until you can go no further. What was the first ancestor's surname? You don't know, because it's all false anyway.

People shouldn't become too attached to being a certain way. The only reason we become afflicted is because of our ego and our selfishness. If we had no ego or selfishness, how could we have afflictions? Why do people lose their tempers? They feel others have done them wrong. When we take a loss, we get angry. When we gain some advantages, we feel happy. In both cases, we are being affected by the situations, due to our ignorance.

A talk given on September 1, 1982
at the City of Ten Thousand Buddhas

BE A GOOD DRIVER

When you have wisdom, you are able to readily solve any kind of problem; when you don't have wisdom, there are obstacles everywhere.

DUE TO THE influence of the six sense faculties—eyes, ears, nose, tongue, body and mind—people are reborn in the hells or become hungry ghosts or animals. It's also due to the functioning of the six senses that people become *asuras* or are reborn in the heavens or as humans.

It is also because of the functioning of the six sense faculties that we can become Arhats, Pratyekabuddhas, Bodhisattvas, or Buddhas. Why are the six sense faculties so powerful that they even influence whether we are reborn in the heavens or fall into the hells? Do they determine whether people become Buddhas or ghosts?

Actually, the six sense faculties aren't in control; it's just that we don't know how to use them. The master is within everyone's own nature, the bright nature of enlightenment. This master is also known as the inherent Buddha-nature. When it is in charge, proper thoughts manifest, and one is free and at ease, not obstructed by anything. But once this nature is covered up by even a single thought of ignorance, a dull darkness is erroneously stirred up; the six sense faculties then become the masters and take control. As a result, we are plundered by the six thieves—the eyes, ears, nose, tongue, body and mind. They rob our house and steal all our precious treasures. So it is said,

> *When not a single thought arises,*
> *The entire substance manifests.*
> *When the six sense faculties suddenly move,*
> *There is a covering of clouds.*

Because of this, people who are supposed to advance along the Buddha path go down the ghostly path instead. This is like a driver who should be driving his car along the highway, but instead drives it into the ocean, both drowning himself and sinking the car. It's also like somebody who aims high without doing the fundamental work, or someone who climbs a mountain and falls off a cliff, getting smashed to bits. When a person is not familiar with the road conditions and doesn't know how to drive, he's prone to accidents. The six sense faculties of our bodies can be compared to cars. If we know how to drive, we can reach our destination safely; if we don't, we risk losing our lives in an accident.

Our inherent nature, which is clear, perfect, and wonderfully bright, pervades the ten directions and permeates heaven and earth. It is omnipotent, capable of doing anything. However, as in the analogy about driving, even though we may know how to drive, once we go into the womb and enter this "stinking skin bag," we become muddled. After this we can't even distinguish between east, south, west, north, above, or below, and run around aimlessly. Originally we wanted to become Buddhas, but if we are the least bit careless, we may end up being reborn as horses, cows, or sheep.

Some Buddhists are most pitiful. They single-mindedly want to leave the three evil paths, but because they don't know how to drive the car of the six sense faculties, they are controlled by them instead, and so they let the demon king get a hold of them. Trapped in this illusory body of the five *skandhas* and incapable of freeing themselves, these people suffer unbearable pain. Their inherent natures have been buried, and the bright light of wisdom cannot manifest.

The myriad things are speaking dharmas. If you understand, they are speaking the Buddhadharma, the transcendental Dharma; if you do not understand, then they are speaking worldly dharma, defiling dharma. In this way everything is contained within a single thought of your mind. When you have wisdom, you'll be able to readily solve any kind of problem; when you don't have wisdom, there are obstacles everywhere.

Our body depends on food to survive. However, this kind of food is coarse. In addition, we also rely on the Buddhanature and the bright light of wisdom to survive. Just as a car needs gasoline to run, people need food and drink to generate energy in order to move. But some cultivators can survive without food or drink. How do they do this? They eat the bright light of wisdom—that is their nourishment.

On a coarse level, our body needs food and drink; on a finer level, our soul need the spiritual nourishment of the Buddha's nature. During the day, when we work, walk, stand, sit, and recline, we exhaust a lot of our energy, use a lot of gasoline. At night when we rest, our pores open up and come into contact with the Buddha light. The bright light of wisdom from the Buddha's radiant treasury enters our pores, replenishing the energy we lost during the day. After we get enough rest at night, our energy returns to its normal level the next day.

Hearing this principle, some people become greedy and think "Oh, so the Buddha shines his light on me while I sleep. Then if I sleep more, will I be wiser?" In reality, we all need a certain amount of sleep. However, if we sleep too much, our brains will become muddled and dull, and our wisdom will be diminished. It's said, "The longer the night, the more you dream." Dreaming also wastes energy. Sleeping too much gives you headaches. So in all things we must know where to stop, and not go to extremes.

Ordinary people don't understand this principle. They think people can survive on just food and drink. But skilled cultivators concentrate on food for the soul. They enjoy sitting in Chan meditation and developing samadhi. By being in touch with the Buddha's wisdom-light, they replenish their energy and increase their wisdom power. But you can't be greedy for meditation, either, or get attached to it. Too much meditation will give you Chan sickness.

We students of Buddhism should not run east and west, seeking outside for some secret dharma, looking for shortcuts, being greedy for bargains, wanting to get enlightened quickly. This will only waste the limited gasoline we have, exhaust us, and diminish our wisdom, and we'll gain nothing. This is the problem with not understanding the principles of fundamental Buddha-dharma and seeking outside for dharmas. What I said today is not a myth. It can be called a spiritual principle. Even the most advanced scientists have not discovered this principle, let alone understood it. They can't even dream of this wonderful doctrine. Basically it's a very ordinary principle, but everyone has overlooked it.

ALL LIVING BEINGS CAN BECOME BUDDHAS

Present living beings are our parents from past lives, and future Buddhas. If you get angry at living beings, this amounts to getting angry at your parents and the Buddhas.

THERAVADA and Mahayana Buddhists have different dates for the Buddha's birthday. Since there are no fixed dharmas, it doesn't matter which day it is; as long as we celebrate with sincerity and worship in a dignified manner, any day can be the Buddha's birthday.

If we spent time investigating these matters, we would just tire ourselves out until our hair turned gray and our eyes became blurred, and we would still not be able to get a definite result. We would only waste a lot of precious time, and that would be a shame.

In Buddhism, people have their own attachments. Some people are attached to Indian Buddhism, some to Sri Lanka Buddhism, some to Chinese Buddhism, some to Japanese Buddhism, and so forth. Having various attachments and views draws boundaries within Buddhism, and thus divides it. Actually Buddhism is boundless and has no limits. I always advocate not drawing boundaries within Buddhism. We should be united and view the world as one family.

I often say, "The Buddhism I talk about is not Indian or Chinese Buddhism, but a Buddhism that pervades empty space and the Dharma Realm." Moreover, within this Buddhism there are no nationalities, no racial differences, no you or me. Not only are people who believe in Buddhism Buddhists, but people who don't believe in Buddhism are Buddhists as well. Why is this so? Because Shakyamuni Buddha once said, "All living beings have the Buddhanature, all can become Buddhas." This confirms that Buddhists are living beings, and non-Buddhists are also living beings.

Someone may insist, "I'm not a living being." If you're not a living being, then what are you? Someone may say, "My name is Heaven. I am Heaven." Don't you know that Heaven is also a living being? Someone may say, "My name is Earth. I am Earth." Don't you realize that Earth is also a living being and is not beyond the scope of living beings?

Living beings dwell in places throughout empty space and the Dharma Realm. Of the ten Dharma Realms, only the Buddha realm is beyond the scope of living beings. Beings in the other nine realms—those of Bodhisattvas, Condition-Enlightened Ones, Hearers, gods, humans, *asuras*, animals, hungry ghosts, and hell-beings—are all within the scope of living beings, and so they're all called living beings.

Since we are all living beings, isn't it fair for me to include non-Buddhists in Buddhism? Such is the big picture of Buddhism. The Buddha said, "All living beings can become Buddhas." Whether you believe in Buddhism or not, you will all become Buddhas in the future, because you are not beyond the scope of living beings. If you don't believe in Buddhism now, you will in the future. If you don't believe in Buddhism in this life, you will in the next one. Eventually, you will believe in Buddhism. Therefore, I regard all living beings as Buddhists.

Some religions assert that there is only one god who created and rules this world or who controls the universe. They maintain that human beings can't become gods; that people can only be god's workers, dominated by him. This theory is the opposite of Buddhist principles.

According to Buddhist principles, everyone can become a Buddha. Present living beings are our parents from past lives as well as future Buddhas. If you get angry at living beings, this amounts to getting mad at your parents and the Buddhas. Thus you become a great rebel and are unfilial. We should be compassionate and respectful towards living beings. We should also treat each other with sincerity, help each other out, and not obstruct or be jealous of one another. This is the greatest aspect of Buddhism.

Regardless of whether or not you believe in Buddhism, and whether or not you have come to bathe the Buddha, I consider all of you Buddhists. If you are Catholic, you're a Buddhist; if you are Protestant, you're also a Buddhist. Even if you are a Jew, a Muslim, or a follower of some other religion, I still regard you as a Buddhist. I will not exclude you from Buddhism. We are all one family. There is no distinction between you and I. See how great Buddhism is! We don't have the notion of excluding other religions.

A talk given on May 9, 1983

AFFLICTION IS BODHI

Having afflictions is having the affliction-ice of ignorance; having no afflictions is having the Bodhi-water of wisdom.

WHEN the Buddha saw that all living beings undergo four great sufferings—birth, old age, sickness, and death—he resolved to leave the home-life, to cultivate and find the way to escape from these four great sufferings.

Without our knowing it, our afflictions manifest themselves. Sometimes they show in our appearance; sometimes they are hidden in our minds. Once ignorance is stirred up, we are totally lost. When ignorance plays its tricks on us, we become muddled. Afflictions are stumbling blocks to cultivating the Way.

On the other hand, we cannot do without afflictions. Why not? Because "affliction is Bodhi." If you know how to use it, affliction is Bodhi; if you don't know how to use it, then Bodhi becomes affliction. Bodhi is analogous to water, and affliction to ice. Ice and water are of the same substance; there is no difference. In freezing weather, water will freeze into ice, and in hot weather, ice will melt into water.

When there are afflictions, water freezes into ice; and when the afflictions are gone, ice melts into water. This principle is very easy to understand. In other words, having afflictions is having the affliction-ice of ignorance; having no afflictions is having the Bodhi-water of wisdom. Please remember this! We shouldn't cultivate for eighty thousand great eons and still have afflictions, day after day living to eat afflictions, and starving to death if there aren't any. That would be truly pathetic.

Where do our sicknesses come from? They come from the three poisons of greed, hatred, and stupidity. If people didn't have these three poisons, there wouldn't be any illnesses. In the Buddhadharma, precepts, samadhi, and wisdom are the antidote to greed, anger and stupidity. They have the magical effect of eradicating sickness immediately upon being taken.

When the mind is clear,
The moon is reflected in the water;
When thoughts are settled,
There are no clouds in the sky.

In this state, there are no afflictions.

When the mind is still and thoughts are gone,
That is true wealth and honor.
When selfish desires are totally cut off,
That is the true field of blessings.

When deluded thoughts are stilled and the exploitation of conditions comes to an end, that is true wealth and honor. In short, to not be greedy is to be wealthy and honored. People are greedy because they aren't content; they feel they don't have enough. Being without selfish desires is called a field of blessings. If the desires are totally cut off, that is the true field of blessings. You should pay special attention to this.

If your mind is at peace,
A hundred difficulties will be dispelled.
If your thoughts are settled,
All things will be auspicious.

This is a famous saying. Use it as a motto, and you will receive limitless benefits throughout your whole life.

What is affliction? Having an afflicted body and an annoyed mind. In this state, there is no self-mastery. What is worry? Distress and vexation, and being in low spirits. What are sudden misfortunes? Accidents and unfortunate events. These things bind you and oppress you, like the lock of ignorance which locks you up, like the rope of affliction which ties you up. They are also like a huge rock pinning you down and suffocating you, so that you cannot breathe. The Buddha wanted all living beings to part with afflictions and attain peace and happiness; to escape from all oppression and gain liberation, and this is why he taught all living beings to bring forth the great Bodhi mind, and to learn and cultivate the Buddha's meritorious, virtuous conduct. Therefore, we living beings should listen to, accept, believe in, and practice the Buddha's teachings.

Living beings' afflictions are limitless and boundless. They are just like a mirage. The Bodhisattvas see how deluded living beings' delusions cause them to reverse the straight and the crooked, black and white, good and evil. No matter how one tries to teach them, they just cannot change their habits.

They have countless layers of obstacles. If you point out their faults, they'll get upset and try to justify them; they don't want to correct them and change for the better. They'll even display great ignorance and become terribly afflicted.

The Bodhisattvas cherish beings with kindness, compassion, and sympathy. Again and again, they remind living beings not to gossip or become afflicted, and tell them that if they don't lose their tempers or let jealousy obstruct them, they'll be able to leave the sea of suffering.

This human body is illusory. Don't always protect this stinking skin bag as if it were a precious jewel, afraid to let it suffer and wanting it to enjoy blessings. In spite of all this coddling, your body only gives you a lot of trouble.

A talk given on May 3, 1983

HOW TO REPAY THE KINDNESS OF THE BUDDHAS AND BODHISATTVAS

From beginningless time, the Buddhas and Bodhisattvas have been giving us their very bodies and lives in order to nurture us.

THE BUDDHAS and Bodhisattvas have come to this world solely for the purpose of teaching and transforming living beings. They use the 84,000 Dharma-doors to gather in beings with whom they have affinities. Failing to understand the spirit of kindness, compassion, joy, and giving of the Buddhas and Bodhisattvas, we turn our backs on enlightenment and wallow in the dust of ignorance. We chase after petty things, forgetting the important things, and don't want to end birth and death or escape the Three Realms.

Everyone knows that the Three Realms are like a burning house; there is no peace within them. Yet we linger in the burning house, not at all scared, and not wishing to leave it, even though we know that it contains nothing but suffering.

The Buddhas and Bodhisattvas explain the Dharma in an effort to teach us, but, unfortunately, we do not understand their intentions. We listen without hearing, and look without seeing; their instructions go in one ear and out the other. We prefer to go on living in a stupor and dreaming our lives away, just like walking corpses. Though we may say we are cultivating, we are not seeking the path of true enlightenment.

How can we find true enlightenment? It's very easy: do not seek outside. All you need to do is turn your back on delusion and return to enlightenment. Turning around from being in the state of delusion is itself enlightenment.

If living beings could renounce their deviant thoughts and return to proper thoughts, they would become enlightened and attain great wisdom. But living beings are not willing to turn back. They prefer to remain bobbing up and down in the bitter sea of birth and death, thinking this sorry state is worthwhile. Confronted with this problem, the Buddhas and Bodhisattvas have no way to enable living beings to leave suffering and attain bliss. Living beings are so deeply deluded that they cannot understand the principles of enlightenment. Their accumulated bad habits are profuse and ingrained, smothering their wisdom. That is why they cannot tell the difference between right and wrong, proper and deviant, true and false.

Once we know what is true, we should leave the false behind. Why are we confused? Because we are bereft of wisdom. Lacking real wisdom, living beings bang their heads against the wall wherever they go: if they are not bumping into the east wall, they are crashing into the west wall, or banging their heads against the north or south wall. Although there is plenty of room in the middle, living beings still insist on running to the four directions to bang their heads against the wall. This is really pitiful!

These poor living beings bash their heads until blood streams down their faces. Yet they still do not know that they need to reflect within. No matter how devotedly the Buddhas and Bodhisattvas work to teach us, setting before us the Tripitaka ("Three Stores") and the Twelve Divisions of the Buddha-dharma, we simply pay no attention. They have bestowed these innumerable Dharma treasures upon us, yet we feel no sense of gratitude; thus the Buddhas and Bodhisattvas feel very tired. Why? Living beings are truly difficult to liberate! The Buddhas and Bodhisattvas exhaust their efforts to save us, yet we remain unmoved; we still go about doing our own things, not cultivating, not upholding precepts. Nevertheless, the Buddhas and Bodhisattvas are not discouraged. No matter how difficult it is to liberate living beings, they still want to do it. They want to compassionately liberate all living beings. How can we repay their kindness? For instance, consider the vows of Earth Store Bodhisattva, who said,

As long as the hells are not empty,
I will not become a Buddha.
Only when all living beings are liberated
Will I become a Buddha.

Everyone should deeply ponder the meaning of these words. Consider how magnificent and great these vows are! Without even reading the Sutra, just by listening to this vow, we should feel deeply indebted to Earth Store Bodhisattva and to all Buddhas and Bodhisattvas for their compassionate and mindful protection of us.

From beginningless time, the Buddhas and Bodhisattvas have been giving up their very bodies and lives in order to nurture us. And so we must bring forth the resolve for Bodhi in order to repay their kindness, as well as the kindness of our parents and teachers and that of heaven and earth. We should seek Buddhahood and vow to liberate all living beings. We should be the Buddhas' compassionate representatives in proclaiming the Dharma and transforming beings, serving society and the country with a sense of righteousness. Let us always be compassionate and righteous, propagating the Buddhadharma and carrying out the Buddha's original intent with our humble effort.

Why is it that after the Buddhas have become Buddhas, they still do not forget living beings and they vow to liberate us? It's because all living beings have the Buddhanature and can become Buddhas. However, living beings do not realize this. Covered up by greed, hatred, stupidity, ignorance, afflictions, and idle thinking, their true wisdom cannot manifest. Therefore, the Buddhas and Bodhisattvas come to show us the way to become enlightened. If we can cultivate accordingly, we will surely attain wisdom. We should remember and be grateful to the Buddhas and Bodhisattvas, as well as our parents and teachers. Human beings are ranked equally with heaven and earth. We should not waste our precious lives. We should clearly recognize the Buddhas' and Bodhisattvas' intent and the power of their vows, so that we don't live our human lives in vain.

A talk given on July 9, 1983

THE WONDERFUL WAY

What is the wonderful Way? It's simply the Way that we practice every day.

THE BUDDHA can perceive the amount of goodness and evil in each living being's disposition. He also knows whether a living being's desires are many or few. Knowing this, the Buddha taught living beings a variety of wonderful ways to practice.

What is the wonderful Way? It's simply the Way that we practice every day. The Way that we practice, use, and experience every day is wonderful. If we don't look into it carefully, we won't perceive its wonder. But careful scrutiny will reveal how everything is wonderful beyond words. For instance, where do the things we use every day come from? Their origin is wonderful. Where do they go? That is wonderful too. In either case, it's the wonderful Way.

The events of our daily life are also the wonderful Way. For instance, when we go without food, we feel hungry. Why? That is wonderful. After we eat, we get full. That is wonderful too. Even getting dressed and drinking tea are wonderful. Otherwise, why would we do them? Even though we engage in these activities, they don't last long. They are only temporary. Wouldn't you say that's wonderful?

"Anyone could understand this principle!" someone is thinking. But your understanding is quite superficial, not ultimate. You haven't seen the wonder of it. Why do people like good food? That's wonderful. Why do they want to wear nice clothes? That's also wonderful. Why do they like to live in fine houses? That's wonderful as well.

Their wonder lies in the fact that we don't understand them. If we understood, it would be wonderful. Since we don't understand, it's not wonderful. For example when one of the "three steps one bow" cultivators was bowing on the highway, his pants ripped open and left his body exposed. Just then a pair of pants appeared on the side of the highway. That was wonderful. When some people threw bottles at them and missed, that was also wonderful. There is too much to say about the wonderful.

A talk given on November 5, 1980

CURE FOR WHAT AILS US

We must cleanse our inherent nature. How? We can use the Six Guidelines—no fighting, no greed, no seeking, no selfishness, no pursuit of personal advantage, and no lying

WHAT ARE the three external evils? They are killing, stealing, and lust. Why is there so much turmoil in society? It's because of the mischief caused by these three evils. Most of the news in the newspaper every day has something to do with these three evils. It is said, "Of the myriad kinds of evil, lust is the foremost." Eight or nine out of ten killings are motivated by lust. This deviant trend is truly horrible. If one doesn't kill, steal, or engage in sexual misconduct, then one is imperceptibly helping to settle the society and maintain peace in the world.

What are the three internal poisons? They are greed, anger, and delusion. With insatiable greed, people are never content. They are happy when they obtain whatever they are greedy for, and angry when they don't. As soon as they get angry, ignorance starts to stir up trouble and encourage fighting. At that time, they lose their sense of reason and become foolish. They act without thinking of the consequences and do muddled things. In a less serious case, they might just hurt people's feelings. In a more serious case, they may do totally outrageous things.

How can we extinguish the three internal poisons? Shakyamuni Buddha left us a good prescription—precepts, samadhi, and wisdom. Cultivators must uphold precepts. When precepts are upheld, samadhi power comes forth. And from samadhi power, wisdom power arises. They are all connected. If one can observe precepts, one will not have greedy desires. If one has samadhi, one will not give rise to anger. If one has wisdom, one will not act foolishly.

The three evils of the body come from our external physical nature. The three evils of the mind arise from our internal psychological nature. Because of greed, anger, and delusion, one commits killing, stealing, and sexual misconduct. If one could convert greed, anger, and delusion into precepts, samadhi, and wisdom, then killing, stealing, and sexual misconduct would no longer occur.

The three poisons defile our inherent nature so that it cannot be clean and pure. When the true mind is covered up, the false mind becomes the host and controls everything. As a result, we are muddled and confused, with never a clear moment. Living this kind of life, one is nothing but a walking corpse. What fun is there in that?

We must cleanse our inherent nature. How? We can use the Six Guidelines—no fighting, no greed, no seeking, no selfishness, no pursuit of personal advantage, and no lying—to wash and sweep until not the slightest bit of filth remains.

With no fighting, the world will naturally be free of wars. Without greed for fame and benefit, people will get along harmoniously. With no seeking, one's character will naturally be lofty and noble and one will be respected by everyone. With no selfishness, one will always be considerate towards others and forget oneself. One won't find fault with others and won't discriminate about the four marks [of self, others, living beings, and life span]. With no pursuit of personal advantage, all benefits will be shared equally and no one will try to monopolize things. One may even go out of one's way to take a loss so as to make others happy. With no lying, people will trust one another and always speak the truth, and thus unnecessary troubles will be avoided.

When we practice these Six Guidelines and bear them in mind, we are indirectly helping the government and directly helping ourselves. We should realize clearly how important our own responsibilities and obligations are. We want to be perfect and outstanding members of the society, not bad citizens who disturb others. If we can be like this, then we are true Buddhists. I hope you will work hard in this respect. If you always go far off seeking for some secret and wonderful dharma, you are losing the substance for the shadow and will never find the true Dharma.

Finally, I hope everyone will cast the three external evils and the three internal poisons far, far away, and never have to deal with them again. These evils and poisons are vile, corrupt, and untrustworthy. If we aren't careful, we will fall into their clutches. They certainly welcome us to be a part of them and wallow in the mire with them. Take care not to get caught in their snares. If we aren't clear about things, we will turn away from enlightenment and unite with defilement, forming a partnership with the six defiling sense objects. We must be alert and wise enough to turn away from defilement and unite with enlightenment.

WHAT IS THE INITIAL THOUGHT?

The initial thought refers to the state of original understanding; it comes from our true mind, our original face.

DISCIPLE: What is meant by the "initial thought"?

Venerable Master: It's the original thought, which understands things without pondering, and without using the sixth consciousness--the discriminating mind. If you think, then you're using the human mind, not the mind of the Way. The initial thought is truth in the primary sense, not in a secondary or tertiary sense.

Disciple: When we see tasty food, our initial thought is to eat it. When we see beautiful objects, we want to possess them. Is that "truth in the primary sense"?

Venerable Master: No. Don't get it wrong. The initial thought refers to the state of original understanding; it comes from our true mind, our original face. Thoughts of greed for food or nice things come from the false mind, the greedy mind, not the true mind. For example, our investigation of true principle here is considered yang while our greedy thoughts for food and good things are yin. The latter cannot be considered truth in the primary sense. It counts only if the mind strives for truth and light. The deciding factor is whether the mind is progressive or degenerative. It should be realized that when people fall into the hells, it also starts with the initial thought, but that thought is deviant, yin, and degenerative in their case, leading them gradually toward the hells. We have to be clear on these basic questions; we can't mix them up.

Disciple: Someone once asked, "Buddhism says, 'A human body is hard to attain. Once you lose it, you may not regain it for ten thousand eons.' If so, why is the population of the world increasing so rapidly right now? Clearly, more people are being born than dying. How does Buddhism explain this?"

Venerable Master: Although the human birth rate is high, how do you know that there aren't more living beings dying than living? These figures cannot be reckoned accurately, nor can they be determined scientifically. They can only be expressed by means of analogy. Once, when the Buddha was in the world, he scooped up a handful of dirt from the ground and said, "Those who have attained a human body are as many as the dirt particles in my hand. However, those who have lost a human body are as many as the dirt particles covering the earth." The population of the world seems unlimited, but how do you know that the number of people who have lost their human form doesn't exceed it infinitely many times over?

There weren't as many human fatalities in the past. Presently, the mortality rate from hurricanes, fires, automobile and airplane accidents, wars, and nuclear explosions is quite high. And it's very possible that the people who died were unable to become human again. They might have been reborn as ants, mosquitoes, or fierce beasts—how could the number of such cases ever be scientifically determined?

How is it that a child is suddenly endowed with feelings and awareness after it is born? This is a very basic question, but ordinary people have overlooked it and not investigated it. Though we are currently experiencing a population explosion, there are more people losing their human form than before. In the past there weren't so many ants, mosquitoes, and other harmful insects. How do you know that these moisture-born, transformationally born, and egg-born living beings didn't come from human beings?

After a person loses his human form, his nature and spirit become fragmented. One person's spirit may be transformed into many animals, perhaps even into 84,000 mosquitoes. Since the person's wisdom has been divided up into many tiny shares, the resulting animals are dull-witted. In order for them to integrate into human form again, they have to be resmelted in the "chemical factory," which may take a long period of time.

Also, people who were married more than once will under the retribution of having their souls split into several parts at the time of death. Abortion is another major problem. An abortion amounts to depriving someone of a human body. Currently, the number of deaths from abortion exceeds the number of living people.

Is it possible for insentient beings to regain their spiritual nature? Yes, if they meet the right person who speaks Dharma to them. An example of this would be how, "When the Venerable Sheng spoke the Dharma, even the dull rocks nodded." They, too, have the opportunity to regain their spiritual nature, but only when they meet up with a Sage or an Arhat.

A talk given on November 10, 1986

WATCH OVER YOUR OWN MIND

Cultivation is the cultivation of singlemindedness. If we can focus our thought on a single point—concentrate on one thing—then we can achieve anything.

BUDDHISM emphasizes the law of cause and effect, the retribution always comes around and is never off by the slightest bit. For whatever cause one plants, one receives the corresponding effect. One who plants good causes will receive good effects; one who plants evil causes will receive evil effects. If you plant the cause of scolding people, you will receive the retribution of being beaten.

If you plant the cause of beating people, in the future you will receive the retribution of being killed. The ancients said, "If you kill someone's father, your own father will be killed; if you kill someone's brother, your own brother will also be killed." As is the cause, so shall be the effect. We living beings are afraid of effects, but not of causes. We are not cautious when planting causes, but we become nervous when the effects appear. In contrast, Bodhisattvas fear causes but not effects. They are very cautious in planting causes; however, when the retribution comes around, they willingly accept it and don't try to evade it. That's the difference between living beings and Bodhisattvas.

A great resolve brings great blessings, while a small resolve brings small blessings. A great resolve is a great cause that will eventually produce a great effect. We should know that "Everything is made from the mind." Therefore, we should refrain from all evil and practice all good. Buddhahood is accomplished from a single thought of the mind. People cannot control their minds. Although the mind is inside the body, it constantly runs outside. Our false thoughts may take us as far away as the heavens or hells, or as close as New York or San Francisco. We have no control over our own minds. Cultivation is the cultivation of singlemindedness. If we can focus our thought on a single point—concentrate on one thing—then we can achieve anything.

A talk given on May 3, 1987
at the University of Oregon

THE BODHI MIND IS THE TRUE MIND

The Bodhi mind refers to the wholesome seeds inherent in every person's mind.

WHAT IS the Bodhi mind? Bodhi is a Sanskrit word meaning "the Way of enlightenment." The Bodhi mind is the fundamental true mind, the unconfused mind. The confused mind is the mind that creates offenses, and thus is not the mind of the Way of enlightenment. Therefore, we must recognize this path and know whether it is an easy or a difficult one to travel. Only when we have truly recognized the path will we be able to reach our destination.

Further, the Bodhi mind is the law that is to be observed whether we are moving or still, awake or asleep. This law refers to the precepts. To put it simply, the law is "To refrain from all evil and practice all good." "To refrain from all evil" is to follow the precepts. There are the five precepts (that prohibit killing, stealing, sexual misconduct, lying, and taking intoxicants.) "To practice all good" means to practice the ten good deeds. Our body, mouth, and mind are capable of ten evil deeds: The body commits the evil deeds of killing, stealing, and sexual misconduct; the mouth utters loose speech, false speech, harsh speech, and divisive speech; and the mind can be greedy, angry, and stupid. If one can refrain from committing the ten evil deeds, one is practicing the ten wholesome deeds.

The body is capable of three evil deeds: killing, stealing, and sexual misconduct. Many people are actually incapable of distinguishing right from wrong. They create offenses knowing full well what they are doing. Take killing, for example. Many people know that killing living beings is wrong, but they still break the precept against killing. Stealing is defined as taking things that are not given. People are fully aware that stealing is bad, yet they still do it. People commit sexual misconduct because they crave the false pleasures of the flesh. People are easily deluded by these false pleasures to the point that they forget about true happiness. Not recognizing what's real, they run after what's false. And so there's a saying: "One can sell ten loads of false merchandise in one day, but can hardly sell one load of genuine merchandise in ten days." People in the world are just that strange!

Our mind has three evils: greed, anger, and stupidity. Greed means being insatiably greedy. Someone may think, "If I had a million dollars, I'd be satisfied. However, when he has the million, he wants ten million, or even ten billion! His greed can never be satisfied. There's a verse that goes like this:

Every day we're busy just to fill our stomachs.
After our stomachs are filled, we want to be clad.
When we have sufficient food and clothing,
We want to have a high rise and a beautiful wife.
After obtaining a beautiful wife and a charming mistress,
We need a ship and a plane so we can go places.

Once the ship and the plane are in our possession,
We still need to have an official post so we won't be bulied.
The fifth and fourth ranks are petty officials;
The third and second ranks are still too low.
After making it to the first rank—the prime minister,
We want to ascend the throne to be the emperor.
Once we ascend the throne and sit in the imperial court,
We wish to become an immortal and play a game of chess.

This verse describes our insatiable greed. Even when one has millions, one wants to control the economy of the nation. After one is in charge of the nation's economy, one wants to control the economic pulse of the world. In any case, there are two kinds of people in this world: one kind is greedy for fame, the other for profit. People who are greedy for fame come up with infinite schemes to maximize their reputation. Those who are greedy for profit rack their brains thinking of ways to make more money. They are all driven by greed.

The mind also has the poison of anger. Anger refers to thoughts of hatred and a big temper. It is said, "One who lacks virtue has a smoking top." A person with a big temper always seems to have smoke coming from his head; he looks furious and ready to explode. This is evidence of a lack of virtue. A truly noble person does not have any temper. Even if he has a temper, he can subdue it and keep his body and mind calm. He can transform the poison of anger into auspicious harmony and turn violence into peace.

The three poisons of greed, anger, and delusion are interrelated. All human affliction comes from greed and desire. When we have greed and desire, we seek outside. When we see something nice, we want it for ourselves. If we cannot get what we want, we get angry. Once we get angry, our mind becomes confused and stupid. The poison of delusion is not the stupidity of a retarded person. It refers to being unreasonable, ignorant of cause and effect, and deluded. These three poisons are the source of all affliction. If we want to get rid of affliction, we must cut off the three poisons of greed, anger, and stupidity.

Our mouth can easily commit four offenses: loose speech, false speech, harsh speech, and divisive speech. Loose speech includes frivolous talk, sarcastic remarks, and indecent talk that causes people to give rise to unclean false thoughts. False speech refers to untruthful words—lies. Harsh speech means berating people so viciously that they cannot take it. Divisive speech refers to spreading gossip and causing discord among people, like a two-headed snake.

The above has been a brief explanation of the ten evil deeds committed by the body, the mouth, and the mind. If we can turn the ten evil deeds into the ten wholesome deeds and carefully observe them without transgression, that is upholding precepts. The Bodhi mind is another name for the precepts. Precepts guide us to enlightenment. The Bodhi mind refers to the wholesome seeds inherent in every person's mind. If we don't forget the Bodhi mind, our good roots will not be cut off. The absence of delusion is itself the Bodhi mind. We should carefully nurture and develop the wholesome seeds of Bodhi and walk on the path to Buddhahood.

A talk given on June 18, 1987

HOW CAN WE DETERMINE OUR OWN DESTINY?

Our human roots are filiality, brotherhood, loyalty, trustworthiness, propriety, righteousness, integrity, and a sense of shame.

EACH OF us should look within and ask ourselves: From the time I was born until now, what kinds of things have I done? Have I done more good deeds or more bad deeds? Have I done benefited others more, or have I harmed others more? We should take stock of ourselves. There is a saying:

> *A superior person knows how to mold his own destiny.*
> *We determine our own fate and seek our own fortune.*
> *Calamities and blessings are not fixed;*
> *We bring them upon ourselves.*
> *The consequences of our good and evil acts*
> *Follow us just like shadows.*

Why is a superior person said to be able to control his fate? Qiu Changchun, the Taoist Patriarch of the "seven truths," was fated to die of starvation, but because he cultivated diligently, not only did he avoid starving, he became the foremost of divine immortals.

Some people are born fated to be poor, but

because they do good deeds, they later become rich. Getting rich is not our final aim, but most people think that a person who strikes it rich must be happy. Why isn't getting rich our final goal? Our final goal is to gain true understanding; then we will not have lived our lives in vain. If you lack understanding, then you can't control your own birth and you are born in a muddle. Nor can you control your death; you also die in a muddle. No matter how much wealth, honor, and status you have, it's of no use. But if you understand, you have freedom over birth and death. If you want to live, you can live to be eight hundred years old. If you want to die, you can die at any time without any problems. That is freedom over birth and death. Obtaining freedom over birth and death is the most important matter. Since ancient times until now, people have overlooked this matter in their pursuit of wealth and high rank. They have lived as if drunk and died in a dream, being muddled all their lives.

No one is aware of this problem. Now in the Space Age, we should look into it. AIDS and cancer are very common in the world right now. Disease is one form of retribution. They indicate that living beings' karmic offenses are extremely grave. Their offenses of killing, stealing, sexual misconduct, and false speech are extremely heavy. The karma created through taking alcohol and other intoxicants is also severe. That's why so many incurable and strange diseases have developed. These are living examples of Dharma that tell people to quickly gain true wisdom and not do such muddled things.

If we can refrain from killing, stealing, sexual misconduct, lying, and taking intoxicants, then no matter what we say, our words will be efficacious. We don't have to speak of practicing, such as chanting mantras or bowing to the Buddhas. If we can uphold these five precepts, then whatever we say will be efficacious.

If people cultivate honestly, then all their problems will be resolved. We first have to do a good job of being people, and then can we think of becoming Buddhas. We should not forget our human roots. Our human roots are filiality, brotherhood, loyalty, trustworthiness, propriety, righteousness, integrity, and a sense of shame. These virtues are the essence of Chinese culture, so even though we are overseas in another land, we Chinese people should be good models for all of humankind. We should doing a good job of being people. We have affinities with each other, so I have spoken to you from my heart.

We shouldn't take money so seriously. Money is no better than dung or dirt. We should base our actions on our Chinese heritage of filiality, brotherhood, loyalty, trustworthiness, propriety, righteousness, integrity, and a sense of shame; and of humaneness, righteousness, the Way, and virtue. These are our human roots.

A talk given on October 22, 1990
at the Overseas Chinese Association in Paris, France

BUDDHA

We should cultivate the Way, and then we can end suffering, cut off afflictions, and attain Bodhi.

WHEN Shakyamuni Buddha was sitting under the Bodhi tree, one night he saw a bright star and exclaimed, "Strange indeed!" three times. He said, "All living beings possess the Thus Come One's wisdom and virtuous characteristics, but because of their false thoughts and attachments, they cannot realize them." Then the Buddha went to the Deer Park to teach the first five Bhikshus, of whom Ajnatakaundinya was one, by turning the Dharma wheel and explaining the Four Noble Truths.

On the first turning of the Dharma Wheel, the Manifestation Turning, the Buddha said:

This is suffering; it is oppressive.
This is accumulation; it is incurred.
This is cessation; it can be realized.
This is the Way; it can be cultivated.

Suffering oppresses people, causing them to undergo endless births and deaths. It is oppressive. But people should know that:

Enduring suffering puts an end to suffering.
Enjoying blessings uses up blessings.

We should accept the suffering we are supposed to receive. After we undergo it, it is over and done with. Enjoying blessings includes eating, drinking, and having fun, wasting our energy as we linger in this world of temptations, being born and dying, not knowing how to return. This is not knowing how to end suffering. In the midst of suffering, we take suffering to be happiness; this is being upside-down.

"This is accumulation; it is incurred." We accumulate and gather afflictions. We bring them upon ourselves within our own minds. When the mind comes into being, all phenomena come into being. When the mind ceases to exist, all phenomena cease to exist. The root of all afflictions is attachment. We incur afflictions because of selfishness and delusion. If you are internally weak, you will contract sickness from the outside. If you didn't have afflictions inside you, you wouldn't attract external afflictions. As the saying goes, "When there is a great man in the house, great men come to the door. When there is a petty man in the house, petty men come to the door." Whatever you have inside of you, that's what you will attract from the outside. That's how afflictions are brought on.

"Living beings are boundless; I vow to save them. Afflictions are endless, I vow to cut them off." Living beings are in the sea of suffering, and we must rescue them. Our afflictions have no end to them, and so we want to sever them. Yet the Sutras say, "Afflictions are Bodhi, and birth and death is Nirvana." If we cut off afflictions, are we cutting off Bodhi as well? Bodhi cannot be cut off, and afflictions don't need to be cut off either. We should turn afflictions into Bodhi, just like ice melts to become water. The ice is affliction, and the water is Bodhi.

Ice is water, and water is ice. If you can recognize your afflictions, you have ended them. If you can't recognize them, they are still afflictions. Cutting off afflictions means turning them around. One side is afflictions, the other is Bodhi; all you have to do is flip sides.

In cultivation, do not seek things that are high and far away, and fail to recognize that the Way is right in front of you. If you seek the Way far away, you are renouncing what is close at hand. If, in your own daily life, you can be aware of everything you do, if you can understand all your habits and faults, and get rid of all your defilements, just that is the Buddhadharma. And so there is a saying:

Everything is easy to deal with,
But a bad temper is hard to change.
If you can really never get angry,
You have a priceless jewel.

If you can also not blame others,
Then everything will turn out well.
If you are never troubled by afflictions,
How can offenses find you?
If you're always looking at others' faults,
Your own suffering hasn't ended yet.

Where can you find a priceless jewel? If you don't have a temper, that is a priceless jewel. If you never bear a grudge, never curse heaven or blame people, then everything will go well. If you get afflicted, then your karmic creditors will come looking for you.

If you never get afflicted, your karmic creditors won't be able to find you. If you spend all your time picking out others' faults and nagging at others morning till night, you're just washing other people's dirty laundry.

"This is the Way; it can be cultivated." Earlier we talked about suffering and afflictions. Suffering oppresses us, and so we bring afflictions upon ourselves. What should we do?

We should cultivate the Way, and then we can end suffering, cut off afflictions, and attain Bodhi. That's why it's said that the Way is something we can cultivate.

"This is cessation; it can be realized." What do we cultivate the Way for? It's for the sake of attaining permanence, bliss, true self, and purity. We want to attain the ultimate, true happiness. It was for the sake of attaining ultimate happiness that Shakyamuni Buddha, when he was a youth cultivating in the Himalayan Mountains in a previous life, gave up his life for half a verse. The story goes like this:

Shakyamuni Buddha's previous incarnation heard a rakshasa ghost reciting a verse:

All things are impermanent;
They are subject to production and extinction.

Everything in this world is temporary; everything comes into being and then ceases to be. Hearing this verse, the Buddha's previous incarnation asked the ghost, "The verse you're reciting should have four lines. You've only recited two lines. Why don't you recite the last two lines for me?"

The ghost answered, "I'm starving. I don't have the energy to recite the last two lines. If you want me to recite them, I have to eat a human being before I can do so."

The Buddha said, "I'm willing to let you eat me. Recite those two verses, and then you can devour me."

The ghost said, "How can I recite it if I don't have any energy?"

The Buddha still pleaded with the ghost. Finally the ghost took pity on him and recited:

> *When production and extinction are extinguished,*
> *That quiescence is bliss.*

There is production followed by extinction, extinction followed by production. When production and extinction are both finished, that quiescence is happiness. After the Buddha heard these two lines, the ghost got ready to eat him.

The Buddha said, "Now that you've recited the verse for me, we ought to preserve it in the world. If we don't, it will be gone. Wait as I carve this verse onto the tree trunk, and then you can eat me." Then the Buddha carved it into the tree. When he was done, the ghost was again going to eat him, but the Buddha said, "I still don't think it's good enough. I should carve this verse into stone. Although it's carved on the tree, the rain and the wind will wear it down until it disappears. If I carve it in stone, it will never be worn away." Then he carved it in stone, and after he was done, he invited the ghost to eat him.

The rakshasa ghost suddenly rose into the air and vanished. It had been a heavenly being coming to test the Buddha to see if he was really free of a notion of self, if he had really put down his body. Then the heavenly being manifested itself and said, "You are a true cultivator of the Way. Not long from now you will attain Buddhahood."

On the second turning of the Dharma Wheel, the Exhortation Turning, the Buddha said:

> *This is suffering; you should know it.*
> *This is accumulation; you should cut it off.*
> *This is the Way; you should cultivate it.*
> *This is cessation; you should realize it.*

On the third turning, the Certification Turning, the Buddha said,

This is suffering; I already know it and need not know it further.
This is accumulation; I have already cut it off and
need not cut it off anymore.
This is the Way; I have already cultivated it and
need not cultivate it further.
This is cessation; I have already realized it and
need not realize it anymore.

That was how the Buddha turned the Dharma wheel of the Four Noble Truths three times in the Deer Park.

A talk given on October 25, 1990
in Grenoble, France

Verse of Transference

May the merit and virtue accrued from this work
Adorn the Buddhas' Pure Lands,
Repaying four kinds of kindness above
And aiding those suffering in the paths below.

May those who see and hear of this
All bring forth the resolve for Bodhi
And, when this retribution body is over,
Be born together in the Land of Ultimate Bliss.

Appendix

Glossary

Index

Biographical Sketch of the Venerable Master Hsuan Hua

Glossary

Afflictions. Klesha in Sanskrit. The many troubles that derive from greed, anger, stupidity, arrogance, doubt, and improper views. [also see 136]

Agama Sutras. These Agama, meaning incomparable Dharma, sutras were spoken early, during the period of Theravada teaching.

Arhat. Shravaka in Sanskrit, which means Hearers, refers to four distinct levels of sagehood, culminating in freedom over physical birth and death.

Asamkhyeyas. Uncountable in Sanskrit.

Ascetic practices. Dhutanga in Sanskrit, meaning to arouse and shake up. The Buddha approved twelve such practices: two deal with clothing, five deal with food, and five deal with dwelling.

Asura. Beings who like to fight. [also see 86]

Attachments. Things that we cling to and can't let go of.

Avatamsaka Sutra. The Flower Adornment Sutra is a major Mahayana sutra.

Bodhi. Enlightenment. [also see 136 & 154]

Bodhisattva Path. In the Mahayana tradition, the process of cultivation that leads to enlightenment.

Bodhisattvas. Enlightened beings who are dedicated to helping other beings become enlightened. [also see 68]

Book of Odes. One of the Chinese classics.

Buddhadharma. The teachings of Shakyamuni Buddha.

Buddha-nature. The potential enlightened wisdom inherent in us all.

Buddha Way. The path that leads to becoming a Buddha.

Chan meditation. Chan (Zen in Japanese) is part of the transliteration of the Sanskrit term dhyana, which refers to stilling one's thought, or quiet contemplation.

Conditioned dharmas. Physical and mental phenomona produced by and reliant upon the mind for their existence. If the mind ceases to create them, such things cease to be.

Cultivation. The process of practice that follows the Buddha's teachings.

Deer Park. Sarnath, the name of a park in Varanasi, India.

Dharma. The teachings of the Buddha.

Dharma body. One of the three types of bodies of Buddhas, which are the Dharma body, the reward body, and the transformation bodies. The Dharma body pervades all places. [also see 67]

Dharma doors. Methods of practice.

Dharma-protecting spirits. See Eight divisions.

Dharma Realm. Dharmadhatu in Sanskrit, this refers to the cosmos, as well as to all noumenal and phenomenal aspects of it. [also see 64]

Doctrine of the Mean. One of the Chinese classics.

Earth Store Bodhisattva. Kshitigarbha in Sanskrit, this Bodhisattva is known for his vows.

Eight divisions of Dharma Protectors. Composed of gods, dragons, yakshas (speedy ghosts), gandharvas (music spirits), asuras (fighters), garudas (great peng birds), kinnaras (music spirits, called questionable spirits because of the horn on their foreheads), and mahoragas (pythons).

Eighth consciousness. The unmoving storehouse consciousness, this is what transmigrates and could be referred to as the soul.

Enlightened by conditions. Those sages who contemplate the life processes from birth to death and thereby become enlightened.

Evil world of the five turbidities. A name for the world we live in. The five are: turbidity of time, views, afflictions, living beings, and lifespans.

Field of blessings. A name given to members of the monastic Sangha, who serve as places where blessings can be planted.

Five dharmas of mantras. These five functions of mantras are: 1) eradicating disasters, Shantika; 2) increasing benefit, Paushtika; 3) subduing, Abhicharaka; 4) hooking and summoning, Akarshani; and 5) venerating, Vashikarana.

Five spiritual eyes. The five spiritual eyes latent in all beings, they are: 1) The Buddha eye, 2) the heavenly eye, 3) the Dharma eye, 4) the wisdom eye, and 5) the flesh eye (different from our two physical eyes.)

Five precepts. The precepts first received by Buddhist disciples, they are restraints regarding: 1) killing 2) stealing 3) lust 4) lying and 5) intoxicants.

Five skandhas. Aggregates that make up the illusory self, they are: 1) form 2) feeling 3) thinking 4) mental formations, and 5) consciousness.

Good roots. The results of beneficial mental, physical, and verbal acts that are founded in faith and nurtured by virtue.

Ghost of impermanence. Harbinger of death, personified as wearing a tall hat.

Ghosts. Beings composed of dark, yin, energy. See hungry ghosts.

Great Brahma Heaven King. Celestial lord of the Brahma Heaven, found in the form realm. [also see 85]

Great Compassion Mantra. The mantra of Guanyin Bodhisattva, it is connected with compassion and healing.

Great vehicle. See Mahayana.

Guanyin Bodhisattva. The Bodhisattva of great compassion.

Hearer. See Arhat. [also see 75]

Hungry ghost. One type of ghost that has a barrel belly and a needle-thin throat, which prevent it from being able to nourish itself. [also see 92]

Ignorance. The fundamental lack of enlightenment. [also see 43]

Karma. Mental, physical, and verbal deeds. Karma comes from the accumulation of causes and resulting effects.

Kumarajiva, Dharma Master. (344-413 A.D.) A renowned monk from India who translated many sutras and lectured on the Dharma in China.

Land of Ultimate Bliss. Amitabha Buddha's unique pure land in the west, based on his 48 vows, where anyone who sincerely recites that Buddha's name can be reborn, taking their karma with them and working it out there instead of in rebirths.

Lapis Lazuli Land. Akshobhya (Medicine Master) Buddha's pure land in the east, based on his 12 vows, where beings can take rebirth.

Lao Zi. Taoist spiritual leader.

Leaving the home life. Initial entry into the monastic Sangha, becoming a novice monk or nun, whereupon training for full ordination is undergone. [also see 124]

Mahaprajnaparamita. The great perfection of wisdom that will take us from this shore of birth and death to the other shore of Nirvana.

Mahayana. The great vehicle as described and taught by Shakyamuni Buddha, that advocates the Bodhisattva Way.

Mantras. The powerful secret syllables of Buddhas and sages that unite dharamas and hold meanings, they are also the names of ghosts and spirits, who are summoned by them to offer protection.

Merit and virtue. Seeing your own nature is merit; equanimity is virtue. Inner

Humility is merit; outer practice of reverence is virtue. Being not apart from one's own nature is merit; correct use of the pure nature is virtue.

Mirror-like Wisdom. One of the four kinds of wisdom realized by Buddhas. The four are: 1) wisdom of having done what should have been done; 2) wonderfully contemplative wisdom; 3) equitable wisdom; 4) Mirror-like wisdom.

Nirvana. There are four kinds: 1) nirvana of one's own nature, which is inherent in us all and can be realized; 2) nirvana with residue, because physical bondage is not yet severed; 3) nirvana without residue, when afflictions and physical bondage are ended forever; and 4) nirvana of no dwelling, when, with wisdom and compassion become interactive, those beyond birth and death stay to help save others.

Outflows. The loss of energy, especially through the senses, that accompanies indulgence in bad habits and afflictions. Outflows are the root of birth and death.

Precepts. Buddhist guides to morality, prescribed by the Buddha to aid us as human beings and in our practice of the Way. [also see 154]

Proper Dharma. The teachings and methods of the Buddha, as opposed to non-ultimate and/or deviant teachings of others.

Rakshasa ghost. Ghosts that devour human beings.

Sage. There are four major levels of sagehood: 1) Buddhas, 2) Bodhisattvas, 3) Pratyekabuddhas, and 4) Shravakas.

Saha world. The world we live in. Saha means capable of being endured, which indicates that suffering must be borne here.

Samadhi. A wholesome state of concentration gained through meditation and other practices.

Seventh consciousness. The consciousness that transmits data back and forth between the sixth (discriminating) to the eighth (storehouse). It is also the ego base.

Shurangama Mantra. This longest and most powerful mantra in Mahayana Buddhism is found in the Shurangama Sutra.

Shramana. A Buddhist monk.

Six paths. The locations of rebirth: 1) hells, 2) hungry ghost realm, 3) animal realm, 4) human realm, 5) asura realm, 6) celestial realm.

Six sense objects. Forms, sounds, smells, tastes, touches, and mental constructs.

Six spiritual penetrations. The penetrations of 1) the heavenly eye, 2) the heavenly ear, 3) the knowledge of past lives, 4) the knowledge of others' thoughts 5) the perfection of spirit, and 6) the cessation of outflows.

Sutra treasury. One of the three treasuries that comprise the Buddhist canon, the Tripitaka. Also see Three Treasuries.

Take refuge. This refers to the formal ceremony in which one can officially become a Buddhist. This is the initial commitment to the study and practice of the Buddha's teachings.

Tao. The Way that leads to Buddhahood.

Ten Dharma Realms. Parts of the cosmic Dharma Realm. [see 64 for details]

Ten good deeds. The three of the body are to refrain from killing, stealing, and lust; the three of the mind are to refrain from greed, hatred, and stupidity; the four of the mouth are to refrain from harsh speech, backbiting, loose speech, and lying. [also see 154-55]

Theravada. The tradition of Buddhism that focuses on individual practice and relies the early teachings of Shakyamuni Buddha. The Theravada and Mahayana traditions share the same moral codes.

Thought delusions. Eight-one categories of delusions that arise when one becomes confused about principle. At fourth stage Arhatship, thought delusions are severed.

Three evil paths. Hells, hungry ghosts, and animals.

Three periods of time. Past, present, and future.

Three poisons. Greed, hatred, and stupidity.
[also see 137, 147, & 155-56]

Three subtle attributes. Attribute of karma, initiating the objective realm; attribute of turning, initiating the false subjective realm; and attribute of manifestations, initiating the world from out of emptiness.

Three Treasuries of the Canon. The three main divisions of the Buddhist canon: the sutras, which discuss concentration; the vinaya, which if the guide to moral behavior; and the shastras, which enhance wisdom.

Triple Jewel. The external Triple Jewel is comprised of the Buddhas, enlightened beings; the Dharma, the teachings of Buddhas; and the Sangha, the monastic community, composed of both ordinary people and sages. There is also the Triple Jewel of our own nature.

Triple realm. The desire realm, the form realm, and the formless realm. Beings in these realms are still subject to birth and death and transmigration in the six paths of rebirth. [also see 82]

Twelve Divisions of the Canon. They are: 1) prose, 2) verse, 3) predictions, 4) interjections, 5) unrequested teachings, 6) causes and conditions, 7) analogies, 8) expanded teachings, 9) records of past lives of the Buddha, 10) records of past lives of disciples, 11) unprecedented teachings, 12) commentaries.

Vajra Sutra. A sutra, excerpted from the Great Prajna Sutra that was spoken by the Buddha in the prajna period, which discusses wisdom.

View delusions. Eighty-one categories of view delusions that arise when one becomes greedy for and fond of when confronted with external states. These delusions are gradually eradicated during the first three stages of Arhatship.

Yin & yang. Dualities that represent male and female, light and dark, strength and softness. [also see 126]

Index

A

B

C

D

E

H

I

J

K

L

M

N

O

P

R

S

T

Biographical Sketch of the Venerable Master Hsuan Hua

The Venerable Master, whose Dharma name is An Tse and style name is Tu Lun, received the Dharma from the Venerable Master Hsu Yun and became the Ninth Patriarch of the Wei Yang Lineage. His name is Hsuan Hua, and he is also called The Monk in the Grave. A native of Shuangcheng County of Jilin Province, he was born on the sixteenth day of the third lunar month in the year of Wu at the end of the Qing Dynasty. His father's name was Bai Fuhai. His mother, whose maiden name was Hu, ate only vegetarian food and recited the Buddha's name throughout her life. When she was pregnant with the Master, she prayed to the Buddhas and Bodhisattvas. The night before his birth, in a dream, she saw Amitabha Buddha emitting brilliant light. Following that the Master was born.

As a child, the Master followed his mother's example and ate only vegetarian food and recited the Buddha's name. At the age of eleven, he became aware of the great matter of birth and death and the brevity of life and resolved to leave the home-life. At fifteen, he took refuge under the Venerable Master Chang Zhi. When he was nineteen, his mother passed away, and he requested Venerable Master Chang Zhi of Sanyuan Temple to shave his head. Dressed in the left-home robes, he built a simple hut by his mother's grave and observed the practice of filial piety. During that period, he bowed to the Avatamsaka Sutra, performed worship and pure repentance, practiced Chan meditation, studies the teachings and comtemplations, and strictly kept the rule of eating only one meal at midday. As his skill grew ever more pure, he won the admiration and respect of the villagers. His intensely sincere efforts to purify and cultivate himself moved the Buddhas and Bodhisattvas as well as the Dharma-protecting gods and dragons. The miraculous responses were too many to be counted. As news of these supernatural events spread far and wide, the Master came to be regarded as a remarkable monk.

Esteeming the Venerable Master Hsu Yun as a great hero of Buddhism, the Master went to pay homage to him in 1946. The Venerable Master Hsu Yun saw that the Master would become an outstanding figure in the Dharma, and transmitted the Dharma-pulse to him, making him the Ninth Patriarch of the Wei Yang Lineage, the forty-sixth generation since the Patriarch Mahakashyapa.

In 1948, the Master bid farewell to the Venerable Master Hsu Yun and went to Hong Kong to propagate the Dharma. He gave equal importance to the five schools—Chan, Doctrine, Vinaya, Esoteric, and Pure Land—thus putting an end to prejudice towards any particular sect. The Master also renovated old temples, printed Sutras and constructed images. He established Western Bliss Garden Monastery, the Buddhist Lecture Hall, and Qixing Monastery. Delivering lectures on numerous Sutras, the Master caused Buddhism to flourish in Hong Kong.

In 1959, the Master saw tht conditions were ripe in the West, and he instructed his disciples to establish the Sino-American Buddhist Association (later renamed the Dharma Realm Buddhist Association) in the United States. In 1962, at the invitation of American Buddhists, the Master traveled alone to the United States, where he raised the banner of proper Dharma at the Buddhist Lecture Hall in San Francisco.

In 1968, the Shurangama Study and Practice Summer Session was held, and several dozen students from the University of Washington in Seattle came to study the Buddhadharma. After the session was concluded, five young Americans requested permission to shave their heads and leave the home-life, marking the beginning of the Sangha in the history of American Buddhism. Since then, the number of American disciples who have left the home-life under the Venerable Master has continued to grow, creating a profound and far-reaching impact on the propagation of the Buddhadharma and the translation of Sutras in the West.

The Master's explanations of Sutras and lectures on Dharma are profound and yet easy to understand. Several decades have passed in a flash, and the Master has ascended the Dharma seat and delivered well over ten thousand Dharma lectures. Over a hundred of his explanations have been translated into English. No one else has overseen the translation of so many Sutras into English. In 1973 the Master established the International Translation Institute, which plans to translate the entire Buddhist Canon into the languages of every country, so that the Buddhadharma will spread throughout the world.

In 1974, the Master purchased the City of Ten Thousand Buddhas and established the Dharma Realm Buddhist University and the Sangha and Laity Training Programs in order to train Buddhist professionals on an international scale. Furthermore, he founded Instilling Goodness Elementary School and Developing Virtue Secondary School in order to save children's minds from corruption. Over subsequent years, the

Master has successively established Gold Mountain Monastery, Gold Wheel Monastery, Gold Summit Monastery, Gold Buddha Monastery, Avatamsaka Monastery, Dharma Realm Monastery, Amitabha Monastery, the City of the Dharma Realm, and other Way-places of the proper Dharma. Dedicating himself to serving others, the Master doesn't mind the toil and suffering. Acting as a model for others in founding schools and expounding the teachings, and in order to promote the talent of future generations, the Master has offered the City of Ten Thousand Buddhas as the "Refuge for the Buddhists of the World." The traditions at the City of Ten Thousand Buddhas are strict, and residents vigorously strive to practice the Six Great Principles established by the Master after he left the home-life: do not content, do not be greedy, do not seek, do not be selfish, do not pursue personal benefit, and do not tell lies. Due to the influence of the Venerable Master's integrity and cultivation, the City of Ten Thousand Buddhas has become an important Buddhist Way-place in the United State. The Master has composed a verse expressing his principles:

Freezing to death, we do not scheme.
Starving to death, we do not beg.
Dying of poverty, we ask for nothing.
According with conditions, we do not change.
Not changing, we accord with conditions.
We adhere firmly to our three great principles.

We renounce our lives to do the Buddha's work.
We take the responsibility to mold our own destinies.
We rectify our lives as the Sangha's work.
Encountering specific matters,
we understand the principles.

Understanding the principles,
we apply them in specific matters.
We carry on the single pulse of the Patriarch's
mind-transmission.

The Venerable Master's profound samadhi and wisdom have truly opened up the great way of Bodhi for living beings in the age of the Dharma's decline. It is as if in the dark night, we suddenly see the lamp of Prajna wisdom, and in the obscurity, we smell the fragrance of the Dharma lineage. It is like a pure lotus which grows out of the mud and blooms. Upon realizing the inconceivable state of a great cultivator, we are moved to express our praise and exaltation.

The Eighteen Great Vows of the Venerable Master Hsuan Hua

1. I vow that as long as there is a single Bodhisattva in the three periods of time throughout the ten directions of the Dharma Realm, to the very end of empty space, who has not accomplished Buddhahood, I too will not attain the right englightenment.

2. I vow that as long as there is a single Pratyekabuddha in the three periods of time throughout the ten directions of the Dharma Realm, to the very end of empty space, who has not accomplished Buddhahood, I too will not attain the right enlightenment.

3. I vow that as long as there is a single Shravaka in the three periods of time throughout the ten directions of the Dharma Realm, to the very end of empty space, who has not accomplished Buddhahood, I too will not attain the right enlightenment.

4. I vow that as long as there is a single god in the Triple Realm who has not accomplished Buddhahood, I too will not attain the right enlightenment.

5. I vow that as long as there is a single human being in the worlds of the ten directions who has not accomplished Buddhahood, I too will not attain the right enlightenment.

6. I vow that as long as there is a single god, human and asura who has not accomplished Buddhahood, I too will not attain the right enlightenment.

7. I vow that as long as there is a single animal who has not accomplished Buddhahood, I too will not attain the right enlightenment.

8. I vow that as long as there is a single hungry ghost who has not accomplished Buddhahood, I too will not attain the right enlightenment.

9. I vow that as long as there is a single hell-dweller who has not accomplished Buddhahood, I too will not attain the right enlightenment.

10. I vow that as long as there is a single god, immortal, human, asura, air-bound or water-bound creature, animate creature or inanimate object, or a single dragon, beast, ghost, or spirit, and so forth, of the spiritual realm that has taken refuge with me and has not accomplished Buddhahood, I too will not attain the right enlightenment.

11. I vow to fully dedicate all blessings and bliss which I myself ought to receive and enjoy to all living beings of the Dharma Realm.

12. I vow to fully take upon myself all sufferings and hardships of all the living beings in the Dharma Realm.

13. I vow to manifest innumerable bodies as a means to gain access into the minds of living beings throughout the universe who do not believe in the Buddhadharma, causing them to correct their faults and tend toward wholesomeness, repent of their errors and start anew, take refuge in the Triple Jewel, and ultimately accomplish Buddhahood.

14. I vow that all living beings who see my face or even hear my name will bring forth the Bodhi resolve and quickly accomplish Buddhahood.

15. I vow to respectfully observe the Buddha's instructions and cultivate the practice of eating only one meal per day.

16. I vow to enlighten all sentient beings, universally responding to the multitude of differing potentials.

17. I vow to obtain the five eyes, six spiritual powers, and the freedom of being able to fly in this very life.

18. I vow that all of my vows will certainly be fulfilled.

Conclusion:

I vow to save the innumerable living beings.
I vow to eradicate the inexhaustible afflictions.
I vow to study the illimitable Dharma-doors.
I vow to accomplish the unsurpassed Buddha Way.

White Universe

The poem "White Universe" was composed by the Venerable Master on February 15, 1972, during a session for recitation of the Six-syllable Great Bright Mantra (Om mani padme hum) at Gold Mountain Dhyana Monastery. The fourfold assembly of disciples sincerely recited around the clock without fatigue, praying for world peace. Upon the completion of the seven-day session, the Venerable Master was inspired to compose this poem. "White Universe" signifies that the entire universe has been purified, so that it is luminous and immaculately white. In order for the universe to be free from defilement, we must cultivate vigorously and begin by "sparing neither blood nor sweat, and never pausing to rest."

Ice in the sky, snow on the ground.
Numberless tiny bugs die in the cold or sleep in hibernation.
In the midst of stillness you should contemplate,
and within movement you should investigate.
Dragons spar and tigers wrestle in continual playful sport;
Ghosts cry and spirits wail, their illusory transformations strange.
Ultimate truth transcends words:
Not thought about or talked about, you ought to advance with haste.
With great and small destroyed, with no inside or out,
It pervades every mote of dust and encompass the Dharma Realm,
Complete, whole, and perfectly fused, interpenetrating
without obstruction.
With two clenched fists, shatter the covering of empty space.
In one mouthful swallow the source of seas of Buddhalands.
With great compassion rescue all,
Sparing no blood or sweat, and never pause to rest!

Buddhist Text Translation Society Publications

http:\\www.bttsonline.org
1777 Murchison Drive
Burlingame, California 94010-4504
Phone: 650-692-5912; Fax: 650-692-5056

When Buddhism first came to China from India, one of the most important tasks required for its establishment was the translation of the Buddhist scriptures from Sanskrit into Chinese. This work involved a great many people, such as the renowned monk National Master Kumarajiva (fifth century), who led an assembly of over 800 people to work on the translation of the Tripitaka (Buddhist canon) for over a decade. Because of the work of individuals such as these, nearly the entire Buddhist Tripitaka of over a thousand texts exists to the present day in Chinese.

Now the banner of the Buddha's Teachings is being firmly planted in Western soil, and the same translation work is being done from Chinese into English. Since 1970, the Buddhist Text Translation Society (BTTS) has been making a paramount contribution toward this goal. Aware that the Buddhist Tripitaka is a work of such magnitude that its translation could never be entrusted to a single person, the BTTS, emulating the translation assemblies of ancient times, does not publish a work until it has passed through four committees for primary translation, revision, editing, and certification. The leaders of these committees are Bhikshus (monks) and Bhikshunis (nuns) who have devoted their lives to the study and practice of the

Buddha's teachings. For this reason, all of the works of the BTTS put an emphasis on what the principles of the Buddha's teachings mean in terms of actual practice and not simply hypothetical conjecture.

The translations of canonical works by the Buddhist Text Translation Society are accompanied by extensive commentaries by the Venerable Tripitaka Master Hsuan Hua and are available in softcover only unless otherwise noted.

Dharma Realm Buddhist Association Branches

The City of Ten Thousand Buddhas
4951 Bodhi Way
Ukiah, CA 95482
Tel: (707) 462-0939 Fax: (707) 462-0949
Home Page: **http:\\www.drba.org**

The City of The Dharma Realm
1029 West Capitol Avenue
West Sacramento, CA 95691 U.S.A.
Tel/Fax: (916) 374-8268

International Translation Institute
1777 Murchison Drive
Burlingame, CA 94010 U.S.A.
Tel: (650) 692-5912 Fax: (650) 692-5056

Women's Translation Institute and Archives Center
1825 Magnolia Avenue,
Burlingame, CA 94010 U.S.A.
Tel/Fax: (650) 692-9286

Institute for World Religions
(Berkeley Buddhist Monastery)
2304 McKinley Avenue
Berkeley, CA 94703 U.S.A.
Tel: (510) 848-3440 Fax:(510)548-4551

Gold Sage Monastery
11455 Clayton Road,
San Jose, CA 95127-5099 U.S.A.
Tel: (408) 923-7243
Fax: (408) 923-1064

Gold Mountain Monastery
800 Sacramento Street,
San Francisco, CA 94108 U.S.A.
Tel: (415) 421-6117 Fax: (415) 788-6001

Gold Wheel Monastery
235 North Avenue 58, Los Angeles, CA 90042 U.S.A.
Tel/Fax: (323) 258-6668

Blessings, Prosperity, and Longevity Monastery
4140 Long Beach Boulevard,
Long Beach, CA 90807 U.S.A.
Tel/Fax: (562) 595-4966

Long Beach Monastery
3361 East Ocean Boulevard,
Long Beach, CA 90803 U.S.A.
Tel/Fax: (562) 438-8902

Avatamsaka Vihara
9601 Seven Locks Road,
Bethesda, MD 20817-9997 U.S.A.
Tel/Fax: (301) 469-8300

Gold Summit Monastery
233 First Avenue West,
Seattle, WA 98119 U.S.A.
Tel: (206) 284-6690 Fax: (206) 284-6918

Gold Buddha Monastery
248 E. 11th Avenue,
Vancouver, B.C. V5T 2C3 Canada
Tel: (604) 709-0248 Fax: (604) 684-3754

Avatamsaka Monastery
1009 4th Avenue S.W.
Calgary, AB T2P OK8 Canada
Tel/Fax: (403) 234-0644

Dharma Realm Buddhist Books Distribution Society
11th Floor, 85 Chung-Hsiao E.Road, Sec 6,
Taipei, R.O.C.
Tel: (02)-2786-3022 Fax: (02)-2786-2674

Dharma Realm Sage Monastery
Tung His Shan Dist#20, Shing Long Tsuan,
Liu Kuei Village, Kao Hsiung Country, Taiwan, R.O.C.
Tel: (07) 689-3713 Fax: (07) 689-3870

Amitabha Monastery
7 Su-chien-hui,Chih-nan Village,
Shou-feng, Hua-lien County, Taiwan, R.O.C.
Tel: (03) 865-1956 Fax: (03) 865-3246

Prajna Guanyin Sagely Monastery (formerly Tze Yun Tung Temple)
Batu 5 1/2 Jalan Sungai Besi, Salak Selatan Baru,
57100 Kuala Lumpur, Malaysia
Tel: 011-(603) 7982-6560
Fax: 011-(603) 7980-1270

Deng Bi An Temple
161, Jalan Ampang,
50450 Kuala Lumpur, Malaysia
Tel: 011-(603) 2164-8055 Fax: 011- (603) 2163-7118

Lotus Vihara Temple
136, Jalan Sekolah, 45600 Batang Berjuntai,
Selangor Darul Ehsan, Malaysia
Tel: (03) 3271-9439

Namo Dharma Protector Weituo Bodhisattva